I0079865

THE NAME THAT CHANGES EVERYTHING

JESUS CHRIST OUR LORD

By

Janet M. Magiera

LWM Publications
Light of the Word Ministry

Versions quoted are noted by abbreviations after the verse citation as follows:

APNT: Aramaic Peshitta New Testament Translation, LWM Publications, 2006.

ESV: English Standard Version, Crossway, a publishing ministry of Good News Publishers, 2001.

KJV: King James Version of the English Bible, 1769 Blayney edition.

LXX: The Septuagint, Brenton Translation, 1851.

NASB: New American Standard Bible, The Lockman Foundation, 1977.

NET: The NET Bible, Biblical Studies Press, 1996.

NIV: New International Version, International Bible Society, 2011.

NLT: New Living Translation, Tyndale House Publishers, 1996.

Copyright © 2025, Janet M. Magiera
ISBN 978-1732662544

LWM Publications, the publishing house of Light of the Word Ministry
6615 Cool Mountain Dr
Colorado Springs CO 80923
www.lightofword.org

Acknowledgements

Every author owes thanks to the people who were involved in the project of writing a book. I am thankful first of all to Susan Dickens who allowed me the use of her photograph for the cover. My editor and dear friend, Trish Moser, was invaluable in searching out the small things that make a big difference in the final version.

Thank you also to Sid Helmus, Jim and Belinda Kaplan, Bob Falk and Dan Connell who support me and encouraged me to finish this project. Special thanks to Bob Falk for his help with the cover.

And most of all, I am thankful to God my Father who has ever been so faithful in my life to continue to teach me and show me so many wonderful things from His Word. It is an honor and privilege to be able to share some of these precious insights with you. And I pray that you as the reader will be able to apply these truths in many different ways.

Table of Contents

Introduction: What is a Word Picture?

Word pictures are a great way to communicate concepts. In English, we normally use illustrations or incidents to endeavor to "paint a picture" that a listener can relate to. For example, if I was teaching about justice, I would describe an incident involving a legal case and the people involved and what the verdict was to try to show whether there was a just handling of the case.

In the Eastern Semitic languages, including Hebrew, Aramaic and Arabic, the illustrations are built into the language itself. There is usually an action verb that is the root or foundation word picture that forms the basis for all the nouns related to that verb. A simple example of how these word families work in Aramaic is one of the words for salvation. The root verb means "to give life to [something or someone]." So the word savior means literally, "life-giver."

In Western languages, we have word families similar to Hebrew and Aramaic, but there are many concepts which do not have an action verb as a root. For example, the word meekness is related to the verb, to be meek or humble, but the concept of meekness is still fairly vague to explain.

While in Bible school in the 1970's, I took an introductory class in Aramaic, using materials that had been developed by Dr. George Lamsa. He was a pioneer in helping to make known the understanding of the Aramaic language to people in the United States. This class started a lifetime adventure for me of studying the language of Jesus and the apostles. What excited me about the class was how picturesque and beautifully simple the language was. Every word picture gave me a foundation to hang my understanding on, as one would hang a coat on a peg so that he could always find it again. (By the way, THAT was how we would explain something in English!)

The Bible was written by Eastern people who lived in an Eastern culture. Understanding the Aramaic text of the New Testament will give us a basis of understanding the culture and from the "flavor" of the language, we as Western people will have a glimpse of the Eastern culture and how the people of the Bible thought.

In linguistics, this difference between the Eastern and Western languages is called dynamic vs. static understanding. Below is a simple chart that shows the differences. Dynamic thinking means that there is an underlying action in the thought. Static thinking is that even a concept is stationary and can be described only with additional unrelated words.

Let's look at some examples.

DYNAMIC	STATIC
Pen – writes letters	Pen – an object with ink
Bible – holy men of God moved by the Holy Spirit (2 Peter 1:21)	Bible – collection of writings or books
God – the strong, mighty leader	God – the name of the Creator
Lord – master, the "boss"	Lord – owner, a title

My book, *The Fence of Salvation*, describes and explains how word pictures work. It is an allegory, an extended metaphor, of some of the basic concepts of Christianity such as love, faith, forgiveness, mercy, justification, sanctification and redemption. These concepts are explained from the Hebrew and Aramaic "word pictures." Each letter of the ancient Hebrew alphabet was originally a picture of something from everyday life that became a stylized pictograph in early Semitic writing. When these pictographs or letters are joined together to form words, the word pictures provide a simple understanding of difficult concepts. The door of life into the fence of salvation is Jesus Christ, the author of salvation. We are connected to the fence by the Spirit of Holiness. And the fence of salvation surrounds believers as a haven of refuge that is rich with God's goodness, care, protection and provision. What an exciting picture of salvation! I encourage you to explore the book on word pictures along with this new one on the names of Jesus.

Chapter 1 – What's In a Name?

In recent years, in the United States especially, parents have begun to name their children with unusual names or with unusual spellings to differentiate them from other children. No longer are there five girls named Mary in a school classroom. This goes along with a great emphasis in our culture on individualism. In contrast, in Biblical times, a name had much more significance than it does sometimes today. Parents considered very carefully the names they would give to their children; often that name had a prophetic implication. An example is with the prophet, Samuel. His name means, "God hears." He was the answer to Hannah's prayer for a child when she was barren, and Samuel grew up to hear God's voice very clearly from a very young age.

When we meet someone for the first time we ask, "What is your name?" and also perhaps, "What do you like to do?" In order to become acquainted with Jesus, I believe learning about his names and character and what he is doing would be a great place to start. A number of years ago I began a study of the names and titles of Jesus. It was extremely revealing! Jesus' names are many and varied. They show his character as well as the ongoing work he continues to do as the risen Lord and Christ as he is seated next to the right hand of the throne of God.

The name Jesus itself is *Yeshua* in Aramaic and is from the root verb *yasha*. When God was talking to Joseph about Mary, he said that his name would be Jesus.

Matthew 1:21 APNT
And she will give birth to a son and she will call his name Jesus, for he will give life to his people from their sins.

WHAT'S IN A NAME?

Yasha means to save, deliver, give victory, or help. Jesus is THE DELIVERER! *Yasha* has the idea of moving from distress to safety or deliverance and requires the help of an outside party, hence a deliverer. This is the essence of the meaning of Jesus' name. The Aramaic word picture of Yeshua is **the power of change completely experienced.**[1]

There is immense power in the name of Jesus - IF we only use it!! People can be healed in the name of Jesus. We can preach in the name of Jesus. Devil spirits must obey the name of Jesus. But why is it important to understand his name? A name, in the Bible, not only shows the character of a person, but also includes his power, authority and purpose. When we truly understand the significance of Jesus' names, we can receive greater answers to our prayers. When, instead of habitually ending a prayer *"in the name of Jesus or Jesus Christ,"* we can actually utilize the power behind his name to have come to pass that for which we are praying. We will see many examples of this in the chapters to come. In addition, there will be *"action items"* to do in each chapter. These items in separate boxes are to encourage practical application of the use of Jesus' names and what they can accomplish.

There is great power in the name of Jesus because there is no greater name that we could claim. Everything must bow to his name.

> *Philippians 2:9-10 APNT*
> *9 Because of this, God also elevated him highly and gave him a name that is greater than all names,*
> *10 that at the name of Jesus every knee should bow that is in heaven and on earth and that is under the earth,*

---

[1] For further explanation, see Janet Magiera, *The Fence of Salvation*, pp. 52-56.

WHAT'S IN A NAME?

In the Eastern culture the idea of doing something in someone's name had great familiarity. A wealthy person could go to the gate of the city and see the list of the debts of another person, take it down, fold the paper in half, and simply sign his name on the outside of the paper. At that point, everyone would know the debts were paid in full in the name of that person because he had the power to clear the debt.

What about our culture? Is there anything which compares to this cultural idea of a name having power?

The power of a name is still true in our culture today. For instance, if I worked for Microsoft Corporation and was given the authority to purchase materials, I would expect delivery of the products I purchased in the name and strength of the company. No one would doubt Microsoft's ability to pay and settle their account. Likewise, if I was given the authority by Bill Gates to call his stockbroker and say, "Buy 10,000 shares of Nvidia at market price," he would immediately place the order because I would be acting for Bill Gates. It would be as if Bill Gates placed the order himself.

It is our job to heal, to preach, to cast out devil spirits, to reconcile people back to God, to have dominion over the world. Jesus Christ has total authority over sickness and death. Therefore, if I say to a person with cancer, "Be healed in the name of Jesus Christ," it will happen, because it is not my own authority or power which does the healing. My job to do as a "worker" or servant of Christ is to put in the request. If I do not perform my job, it would be as though I were in the Purchasing Department of Microsoft but never picked up the phone to place an order. Our request or demand is backed up by the most powerful "company" that ever was.

Now we can read some of the verses about the name of Jesus and understand it in our culture, just like the people in Biblical times understood it in theirs. That is the reason Peter, John, and all the apostles did signs, miracles, and wonders wherever they went in the book of Acts – they used the name of Jesus Christ. They understood the power behind the name.

All things (circumstances, people, conditions) must bow before the name of Jesus. The first thing that is available is remission of sins and the receipt of the gift of the Holy Spirit.

> *Acts 2:38 APNT*
> *Simon said to them, "Repent and be baptized, each one of you, in the name of the LORD Jesus for the forgiveness of sins, so that you will receive the gift of the Holy Spirit."*

Healing is also available for any kind of physical condition. The following passage is about the man who was lame from his mother's womb and was laid daily at the gate of the temple.

> *Acts 3:6 APNT*
> *Simon said to him, "I have no gold and silver, but what I have I will give to you. In the name of Jesus Christ the Nazarene, rise up [and] walk."*

It was faith in the name which gave the man his healing. At the name of Jesus Christ every situation had to bow. Therefore, it only remained for the man to believe and claim his healing in the name of Jesus Christ.

> *Acts 3:16 APNT*
> *And by the faith of his name he has strengthened and healed this [man], whom you see and know, and faith that is in him has given him this wholeness before all of you.*

14

Devil spirits must flee and leave in the name of Jesus Christ. In Acts 16 there was a damsel who was possessed with the spirit of divination and was following Paul, crying out, "These men are the servants of the Most High God..." She was making a general nuisance of herself, so finally Paul cast out the spirit.

> *Acts 16:18 APNT*
> *And so she did many days. And Paul was provoked and said to that spirit, "I command you in the name of Jesus Christ to come out of her." And immediately it went away.*

So far, we have seen that power is available in the name of Jesus Christ. Then also, all manner of healing of body and spirit is available in the name of Jesus Christ.

Another illustration from our culture is the use of a power of attorney. A power of attorney (POA) is a legal document that gives another person the legal right to use his name. Jesus gave us the legal right to sign his name on all our prayers and petitions. Before his suffering and then resurrection, Jesus told the disciples they would be able to ask things in his name.

> *John 14:12-14 APNT*
> *12 Truly, truly I say to you, whoever believes in me, these works that I do, he also will do and more than these will he do, because I go to the Father.*
> *13 And whatever you ask in my name, I will do for you, so that the Father will be glorified by his Son.*
> *14 And if you ask of me in my name, I will do [it].*

> *John 16:24 APNT*
> *Until now you have not asked for anything in my name. Ask and you will receive, so that your joy may be full.*

Colossians then tells us that our whole lives are to be lived in the name of the Lord Jesus.

> *Colossians 3:17 KJV*
> *And whatsoever ye do in word or deed, do all in the name of the Lord Jesus, giving thanks to God and the Father by him.*

Whatever we do should be done in the name of Jesus Christ. The primary thing we should be doing is giving thanks to God by him. What a simple way of life for us! We have all power and authority because of "working for" the most important man in the world, Jesus Christ. When we order anything to be done, it will come to pass. We do not have to worry about our own names and how little they stand for, because we have the right to use the name of Jesus, the Deliverer. People can have salvation and all manner of healing in the name of Jesus Christ. That brings great thankfulness to God for what He has made available in the name of Jesus Christ!

ACTION ITEM: Prayer of thankfulness
Thank you, Father, that you have made available the legal right and privilege to use the name of our Deliverer. Help us to grasp the depth and power of being able to use the name of Jesus.

E.W. Kenyon in his book called *The Wonderful Name of Jesus* sums up this introduction quite well:

> ...We have a right to use His Name! and so in that Name we act representatively, legally.
> This glorifies the Father; this magnifies Jesus; this answers the need of humanity.

Here is supernatural power that is available to every believer.

It is not a question of education or ordination but merely a question of my apprehending my own true position in Christ, and there using the power that has been legally given to me and to every believer.

Oh, the wonder and grace of God![2]

---

[2] E.W. Kenyon, *The Wonderful Name of Jesus,* p. 21.

Chapter 2 – Jesus Christ our Lord

Many titles and names and symbols are used to describe the Son of God, Jesus. Some have said that there are up to 700 different ones. Jesus (Yeshua), Christ (the Messiah) and Lord (Master) are the three main names that we need to understand and most of the titles about him can be put under these three categories. The chapters of this book are divided into these three sections and appropriate names or titles are explained in the categories. Each category shows who Jesus is and shows his character and his ongoing work today. They also show our relationship with him and what our ongoing work should be. These three names also encompass the *"whole armor of God"* from Ephesians 6:10-17. We are to *"put on the new man"* (Ephesians 4:24) and also to *"put on the Lord Jesus Christ"* which is the armor of light.

> *Romans 13:11-14 APNT*
> *11 And also know this, that it is the time and the hour that from now on we should be awakened from our sleep. For now our life has come nearer to us than when we believed.*
> *12 Then the night is passed and the day is near. So we should lay aside from us the works of darkness and we should put on the armor of light.*
> *13 And we should walk in this manner, as in the day, not reveling and not in drunkenness and not in a defiled bed and not in envy and in strife.*
> *14 But put on our Lord Jesus Christ and do not have regard for the desires that are in your flesh.*

JESUS – *Yeshua*

Yeshua is the name we have explained in Chapter 1 as the Deliverer. He is also the Savior and Redeemer in that he gives eternal life to those who believe on him.

> *Ephesians 2:4-7 APNT*
> *4 But God, who is rich in his mercies, because of his great love [with] which he loved us,*
> *5 while we were dead in our sins, gave us life with Christ and, by his grace, redeemed us*
> *6 and raised us with him and seated us with him in heaven in Jesus Christ,*
> *7 so that he could show to the ages that are coming the greatness of the wealth of his grace and his goodness that is to us in Jesus Christ.*

We will discuss Jesus' ongoing work today of deliverance, giving life, forgiveness of sins, care and protection in the titles of "Son of God, Firstborn, Unique and Beloved," "Good Shepherd," and "Mediator/Advocate."

CHRIST – *Meshikha*

When Jesus asked the disciples who they thought he was, Peter answered in Matthew 16:16: "You are the Christ, the son of the living God." Christ means the "anointed one." First, we need to explain what that means.

> *Acts 10:38 APNT*
> *concerning Jesus, who was from Nazareth, whom God anointed with the Holy Spirit and with power. And this is he who traveled around and healed those who were oppressed by the Evil [one], because God was with him.*

We can see several things right away without knowing anything about the word "anointed." God anointed Jesus with 1) Holy Spirit and 2) power. And the result was healing and deliverance from the oppression of the Evil One. Then it says, "because God was with him."

19

The basic idea of anointing in the Old Testament culture is a hygienic practice of applying oil or grease to soften and protect the skin in a dry climate. It can be used of pouring or smearing. This would be very soothing and refreshing. Oil and grease were also used to protect wounds and aid in their healing. In one place the verb is used of oiling a leather shield to keep it from cracking (Isaiah 21:5), and in another place it refers to painting a house (Jeremiah 22:14).

The specific practice of anointing by pouring oil on the head was used as a symbolic act for officially designating and setting apart a person for a certain, public, leadership function in the community. It was a one-time event much like an inauguration or ordination. Things could also be sanctified or dedicated to a special purpose for God by anointing. The three kinds of leaders anointed for their ministries in the Old Testament were priests, kings and prophets. A major difference between Israel and the other nations was that when God had someone anointed or authorized for leadership, he also provided the empowering of the Holy Spirit to do the job.

Thus an "anointed one" in the Old Testament was an authorized and empowered leader. It is interesting to note that Cyrus, the Persian king in Isaiah 45:1 is called by God "my anointed" or messiah, meaning God had chosen him to accomplish a part of his plan whether he was a believer or not. The ultimate anointed king in the line of David, who was promised by God to come and accomplish salvation came to be called the *Mashiach* (in Hebrew) or the *Meshikha* (in Aramaic).

Mashiach comes from the verb to anoint and is spelled *mashach* in Hebrew and *meshakh* in Aramaic. It is a three-letter root: *mem—sheen—kheth*. I call this a "water word" because the first letter of the word is *mem*, and the pictograph of *mem* means water. *Mem* even looks like water (see Master Chart of Pictographs). Water stands for the life that is given by means of the water and can be understood as what the water produces.[3] Jesus was anointed with the Holy Spirit as we already saw and it saturated him. It also set him apart to be able to provide spiritual water and do things with that Spirit. Jesus summarized some of these effects of the Spirit in Luke 4 at the opening of his ministry.

> *Luke 4:18 ESV*
> *The Spirit of the Lord is upon me, because he has anointed [saturated] me to proclaim good news to the poor. He has sent me to proclaim liberty to the captives and recovering of sight to the blind, to set at liberty those who are oppressed,*

Men and women in the Old Testament were given the Holy Spirit as a gift to them, but there were different amounts for different people. Jesus, the Anointed One, had the fullest amount of Spirit ever given to anyone before.

> *John 3:34 ESV*
> *For he whom God has sent utters the words of God, for he gives the Spirit without measure.*

Now we come to see a word which will tie all the understanding together. That is the word *"measure."* The verb in Aramaic, *meshakh*, is a homonym. That means it has two meanings depending on the context of the use. It is similar to our English word bank. Depending on the context, we understand bank to be either a place where money is or the edge of a river. The first meaning of the verb is to saturate,

---

[3] For further explanation, see Janet Magiera, *The Fence of Salvation*, pp. 130-133.

21

pour, but the second meaning is to measure. Since all the nouns formed from this root are related to the verb, some nouns also mean measure. The noun, measure, in Aramaic is spelled *meshukhtha*. See how close it is to *meshikha*, or Christ? The anointing is the full measure of the Spirit that was in Jesus, the Anointed One. This becomes clear in Ephesians.

> *Ephesians 4:7 APNT*
> *Now to each one of us is given grace according to the measure [meshukhtha] of the gift of Christ [meshikha].*

> *Ephesians 4:13 APNT*
> *until we all become one in the faith and in the knowledge of the Son of God and one mature man, in the measure [meshukhtha] of the standing of the fullness of Christ [meshikha].*

God not only anointed Jesus with the full amount of the Spirit, but then he gave it to us as a gift. We have the full measure of the anointing that was on Jesus!

> *2 Corinthians 1:21-22 ESV*
> *21 And it is God who establishes us with you in Christ, and has anointed us,*
> *22 and who has also put his seal on us and given us his Spirit in our hearts as a guarantee.*

And not only that, but we also never lose this anointing. It abides in us, as it did in Jesus. It is not something that comes and goes. What does change, is an individual's demonstration of the Holy Spirit's anointing. All Christians are anointed, meaning they are all authorized and empowered agents of God.

1 John 2:27 APNT
And you also, if the anointing that you have received from him remains with you, will not need anyone to teach you. But as the anointing is from God, it teaches you about everything and it is the truth and there is no falsehood in it. And as he has taught you, remain in him.

What is the purpose of the anointing? To do the same works that Jesus did with power and authority! Heal the sick, raise the dead, and proclaim liberty to the captives! The same power that God anointed – saturated Jesus with – is OURS. Now we know what it is to have *"Christ in us, the hope of glory"* – it is the full measure of the Spirit of God in Jesus. Let us walk according to that full measure and never doubt we can provide that life-giving water to anyone in need.

The chapters on the Messiah are about Christ's ongoing work today of pouring out grace and peace, healing, interceding, and counseling: *"His Name is Wonderful,"* *"Counselor,"* *"Jesus the Prophet"* and *"Prince of Peace."*

LORD – *Adon/Marya*

Lord is *Adon* in Hebrew and *Marya* in Aramaic. The simple word picture of *Adon* is **the strong one of the door of life**.

The root verb *adn* is assumed from the noun and is not used in the Old Testament. The meaning of the root verb *adn* is disputed, but can mean *"to make firm"* or *"to determine, command or rule."* There is a related noun, *eden*, which means base or foundation. This word is used to describe the base of the tabernacle into which the planks and pillars were inserted. It implies solidity. In like manner, *adon* emphasizes that the lord, whether God or a man, provides a door or entrance to continuous life. A lord provides a foundation for life. And of course, Jesus is the greatest Lord, as the phrase, "Lord of lords" emphasizes.

Marya has the letter *mem* again and it means spiritual water or life. A lord or master brings life to those he takes care of. The word picture is basically **spiritual life to the man**. In the New Testament, often Jesus is called Master, or our Lord (*Maran*) or my Lord. He, as the risen Lord, gives life to his brothers and sisters who believe on him. Then he has become our "boss" or master, and we are to follow his lead in his ongoing ministry today of leading, strengthening, teaching and providing a foundation for life.

The chapters in this section are "The Captain of Salvation," "The Breaker," "The Branch of the Lord," "The Light of the World" and "The Last Adam."

Of course, these are not the only names and titles ascribed to Jesus. But as we will see, they are key ones that we can utilize in our daily walk.

ACTION ITEM: Study the summary chart of what the titles Jesus, Christ and Lord show he is doing today.

Jesus	Christ	Our Lord
deliverance, giving life, forgiveness of sins, care and protection	pouring out grace and peace, healing, counseling, interceding	leading, strengthening, teaching, showing the path

---

Chapter 3 – Son of God: Firstborn, Unique and Beloved

Jesus' names are many and varied and show his character as well as the ongoing work that he is still doing as the risen Lord and Christ next to the right hand of the throne of God. We will explore his name as the Son of God in this chapter. Although Jesus has a human lineage through Mary, his true lineage is heavenly. When the angel told Mary she was going to have a child, she was told that he would be called the Son of God.

Luke 1:35 APNT
The angel answered and said to her, "The Holy Spirit will come and the power of the Most High will overshadow you. Because of this, the one who is begotten in you will be holy and will be called the Son of God."

Jesus' lineage is heavenly in four aspects. The first aspect from the above verse is holy. The angel said that the child would be *"begotten"* in Mary. In other words, she would receive the perfect seed from God. When Jesus was baptized, he received the second aspect: Spirit.

John 1:32-34 APNT
32 And John testified and said, "I saw the Spirit coming down from heaven as a dove and it remained on him.
33 And I did not know him, but he who sent me to baptize with water said to me, 'Him on whom you see the Spirit come down and remain, this [one] will baptize with the Holy Spirit.'
34 And I have seen and testify that this is the Son of God."

The third aspect is power. When Jesus was raised from the dead, God made him known as filled with power. This power was from the resurrection and included his new spiritual body.

SON OF GOD: FIRSTBORN, UNIQUE AND BELOVED

> *Romans 1:3-4 APNT*
> *3 concerning his Son, who was born in the flesh of the seed of the house of David*
> *4 and was made known [as] the Son of God by power and by the Holy Spirit, who raised Jesus Christ our Lord from the dead,*

The fourth aspect is that Jesus received eternal life – spiritual life – and now is able to give that life to everyone who believes on his name.

> *John 20:31 APNT*
> *But even these [things] were written that you would believe that Jesus is the Messiah, the Son of God, and [that] when you believe, you would have eternal life through his name.*

FIRSTBORN

God appointed Jesus as the heir of all things and made him higher than the angels. Then he calls him the *"firstborn."*

> *Hebrews 1:2-6 APNT*
> *2 And in these last days, he has spoken to us by his Son, whom he appointed heir of everything and by whom he made the ages,*
> *3 who is the radiance of his glory and the image of his being and almighty by the power of his word. And in his person, he accomplished the cleansing of our sins and sat down at the right hand of majesty in the high places.*
> *4 And this [one] is greater than the angels in every way, even as the name that he inherited is greater than theirs.*
> *5 For to which of the angels did God ever say: YOU ARE MY SON, THIS DAY I HAVE FATHERED YOU, and*

again, I WILL BE A FATHER TO HIM AND HE WILL BE A SON TO ME?
6 And again, when he brought the firstborn into the world, he said: LET ALL THE ANGELS OF GOD WORSHIP HIM.

Jesus is the firstborn of many brothers. Here are just a few verses which show this.

Romans 8:29 APNT
And from the first he knew them and marked them out with the likeness of the image of his Son, that he would be the firstborn of many brothers.

Colossians 1:15, 18 APNT
15 who is the image of the God who is not seen and the firstborn of all created [ones].
18 And he is the head of the body, the church, for he is the beginning and the firstborn from the dead in order that he would be the first in all [things].

Revelation 1:5 APNT
and from Jesus Christ, the faithful witness, the firstborn of the dead and the ruler of the kings of the earth, who loved us and released us from our sins by his blood.

THE UNIQUE ONE

Other titles call Jesus the "Son of the Father" (2 John 3), "Son of the Most High" (Luke 1:32), "Son of the Most High God" (Mark 5:7), "Son of the living God" (John 6:69) and "Son of the Blessed One" (Mark 14:61).

SON OF GOD: FIRSTBORN, UNIQUE AND BELOVED

But another title about his sonship is *"only begotten."* In Aramaic, this means *"only"* or *"unique one."* Jesus is the son of the Father in a completely unique way. Thus, he is the *"only son."* In my Aramaic Peshitta New Testament translation, I use *"unique Son"* for what is translated *"only begotten"* in the King James Version.

> *John 3:16-18 APNT*
> *16 For God so loved the world, even that he would give his unique Son, that whoever will believe in him will not be destroyed, but will have eternal life,*
> *17 for God did not send his Son into the world to condemn the world, but to give life to the world by his hand.*
> *18 He who believes in him is not judged and he who does not believe is judged already, because he does not believe in the name of the unique Son of God.*

Jesus was unique because his conception was miraculous. The Aramaic word for unique is *yikhidaya* and the root verb means to unite. It could be translated unique, unparalleled, incomparable, darling or only. Jesus is united with the Father in an unparalleled way!

> *John 1:18 APNT*
> *No man has ever seen God. The unique one [of] God, who was in the bosom of his Father, has declared [him].*

There is a word play in this verse in Aramaic: in the bosom *(b'auba)* of his Father *(d'abuhi)*. Do you see the form of the word *"Abba"*? Isaac was also a miraculous *"only son"* who is the type of Jesus being the son who is resurrected from the dead. *"Only son"* in Hebrew is *yachiyd*, similar to the Aramaic word.

SON OF GOD: FIRSTBORN, UNIQUE AND BELOVED

> *Genesis 22:1-2, 12 ESV*
> *1 After these things God tested Abraham and said to him, "Abraham!" And he said, "Here I am.'*
> *2 He said, "Take your son, your only son Isaac, whom you love, and go to the land of Moriah, and offer him there as a burnt offering on one of the mountains of which I shall tell you."*
> *12 He said, "Do not lay your hand on the boy or do anything to him, for now I know that you fear God, seeing you have not withheld your son, your only son, from me."*

We now have life because of Jesus being the only begotten of the Father. And we become *"unique"* sons of the Father, too, because of our spiritual birth.

> *1 John 4:9 APNT*
> *By this the love of God toward us is known, because God sent his unique Son into the world that we would have life by him.*

BELOVED SON

There are two different occasions in the Gospels when a voice from heaven says, *"This is my beloved Son in whom I am well pleased."* An earthly father in Biblical times would have said those words at the time of the son's Bar Mitzvah. That phrase literally means *"son of accountability."* At that time, the father invites the son into the family business and he begins his apprenticeship. We do not have a record in the Gospels that there was a voice from heaven. But we do know that in Luke 2:49 when Jesus was in the temple, he remarks to his earthly father when they were searching for him: *"Did you not know that I must be about my Father's business?"*

SON OF GOD: FIRSTBORN, UNIQUE AND BELOVED

The first time a voice came from heaven is at his baptism and the receiving of the Holy Spirit and the start of his ministry.

> *Luke 3:22 APNT*
> *and the Holy Spirit came down on him in the likeness of the form of a dove. And a voice came from heaven that said, "You are my beloved Son in whom I am pleased."*

Jesus was about 30 years old at the start of his ministry. This time when the Lord says this to him, it is a quotation of Psalm 2 where he is installing his king on the holy hill of Zion. Some texts of Luke 3:22 actually add the phrase, "today I have begotten you."

> *Psalm 2:6-8 ESV*
> *6 "As for me, I have set my King on Zion, my holy hill."*
> *7 I will tell of the decree: The LORD said to me, "You are my Son; today I have begotten you.*
> *8 Ask of me, and I will make the nations your heritage, and the ends of the earth your possession.*

The baptism is not only about Jesus being filled with the Holy Spirit, but also that God was saying that he was ready to go forward to do his Father's business and do what he had been preparing for since the time of his Bar Mitzvah. He was ready to go forward! It was as if he said, "I bestow on him now all my riches, power and authority so he might act on my behalf."

The second time is at the transfiguration on Mount Tabor with Peter, James and John.

SON OF GOD: FIRSTBORN, UNIQUE AND BELOVED

Luke 9:34-35 APNT
34 And when he said these [things], a cloud came and overshadowed them. And they were afraid when they saw that Moses and Elijah entered into the cloud.
35 And a voice came from the cloud that said, "This is my beloved Son. Hear him."

Some manuscripts and other gospels add, "in whom I am pleased" and "my chosen one."

Luke 9:35 NET
Then a voice came from the cloud, saying, "This is my Son, my Chosen One. Listen to him!"

Jesus ministers in a completely different way after this point. He begins to act as the high priest. The transfiguration is a glimpse for the apostles into the glory that Jesus would have in the future. In the vision, Moses and Elijah explain what he would need to do to be the Messiah, having to suffer first, before he could be glorified.

2 Peter 1:17-19 APNT
17 For after he received honor and glory from God, the Father, when a voice came to him that [was] like this from glory, splendid in its greatness, "This is my beloved Son, in whom I am pleased,"
18 we also heard this voice from heaven that came to him, when we were with him on the holy mountain.
19 And we also have a word of prophecy that is certain, which you do well when you look at it (as to a lamp that shines in a dark place until the day should dawn and the sun should rise) in your hearts,

We are born again, unique and beloved sons of God, too.

SON OF GOD: FIRSTBORN, UNIQUE AND BELOVED

1 John 3:1-2 APNT
1 And see how great [is] the love of the Father toward us, because he has called us, even made us, sons. Because of this, the world does not know us, because it did not even know him.
2 My beloved [ones], now we are the sons of God and it does not yet appear what we are going to be, but we know that when he is revealed, we will be in his likeness and we will see him as he is.

ACTION ITEM: Honor the Son of God
Lord, we honor you today because you are the firstborn of many brothers and the unique and beloved Son. We acknowledge you as our elder brother and thank you for giving us the privilege of being called beloved also.

Because we are beloved sons also, let's get busy doing the Father's business!

2 Thessalonians 2:13 APNT
But we are indebted to give thanks to God always for you, our brothers, beloved of our Lord, because God chose you from the beginning to life by the holiness of the Spirit and by the faith of the truth.

Chapter 4 – The Good Shepherd

In this chapter we are going to look at Jesus as the good shepherd and how we can use Jesus' name in prayer and access that shepherding for ourselves as well as others. God is THE Shepherd, Jesus is the good shepherd and pastors are under-shepherds of them both. We will also explore how to rely on the shepherd for providing for all our needs.

The Hebrew word for *"to shepherd"* is *ra'ah*. Definitions for *ra'ah* are to feed, tend, watch or shepherd. Feeding refers to an action on our part. But when the definition is tending, then it refers to how God and Jesus tend us. The shepherd is the one who does the tending, the caring, the watching and bringing the sheep to the pasture. The idea of watching implies a lot of different elements, not just a static standing and looking, but all the elements of tending and caring for the sheep. He also takes care of, protects and heals them if necessary.

Why are people compared to sheep? Wouldn't another animal be a better example?

> Sheep can't protect themselves; they don't have sharp teeth, claws or horns.
> Sheep flee from danger and don't help other sheep out.
> Sheep get focused on what is right in front of them – the next patch of grass.
> Sheep tend to wander around trying to find water and food to eat.
> Sheep are afraid of predators like wolves and bears.

To get a sheep to lie down the shepherd must make sure the following four requirements are met:

1. They must be free from all fear.

2. They must be free from friction from others within the flock.
3. They must be free from torment by flies or parasites.
4. They must be free from hunger.

How does a shepherd tend people? We will first look at some of the verses about shepherds from the Old Testament. The most famous is, of course, Psalm 23.

Psalm 23 NLT
1 The Lord is my shepherd; I have all that I need.
2 He lets me rest in green meadows; [causes me to lie down because I am fed and not afraid] he leads me beside peaceful streams [waters of quietness].
3 He renews my strength. He guides me along right paths, bringing honor to his name.
4 Even when I walk through the darkest valley, I will not be afraid, for you are close beside me. Your rod and your staff protect and comfort me.
5 You prepare a feast for me in the presence of my enemies. You honor me by anointing my head with oil. My cup overflows with blessings.
6 Surely your goodness and unfailing love will pursue me all the days of my life, and I will live in the house of the Lord.

ACTION ITEM: Let us take a moment and confess or declare out loud what Jesus will do as our shepherd, and make it personal. The Lord is MY shepherd. I do not want for any care. I do not want for healing. I do not want for strength. I do not want for ability. I do not want for any provision. My shepherd is supplying all my needs.

Some of the key things a shepherd does in Psalm 23 are: the shepherd causes the sheep to lie down and drink from quiet waters, he guides the sheep on right paths, protects and leads them with his rod and staff, heals them with oil and pursues them with love and kindness.

David was a great example of a shepherd leader and king.

> *Psalm 78:70-72 ESV*
> *70 He chose David his servant and took him from the sheepfolds;*
> *71 from following the nursing ewes he brought him to shepherd Jacob his people, Israel his inheritance.*
> *72 With upright heart he shepherded them and guided them with his skillful hand.*

The Hebrew can literally be translated, "and he shepherded them according to the integrity of his heart and with the understanding of his hands he led them." David shepherded Israel with integrity and with understanding. That wisdom came from his desire to seek God's understanding. Shepherds feed people with wise insight.

> *Jeremiah 3:15 ESV*
> *And I will give you shepherds after my own heart, who will feed you with knowledge and understanding.*

Shepherds gently lead the flock so that they are not afraid.

> *Jeremiah 23:4 ESV*
> *I will set shepherds over them who will care for them [feed them], and they shall fear no more, nor be dismayed, neither shall any be missing, declares the LORD.*

THE GOOD SHEPHERD

Jesus is the good shepherd. We need to examine the passage in John 10 where he calls himself that and I believe it will show us four specific things that the shepherd does for his flock.

    1. The shepherd leads the sheep.

John 10:1-5 APNT
1 Truly, truly, I say to you, whoever does not enter the sheepfold of the flock by the gate, but climbs up by another place, that [man] is a thief and a robber.
2 But he who enters by the gate is the shepherd of the flock,
3 and for this [man], the keeper of the gate opens the gate. And the flock hears his voice and he calls his sheep by their names and leads them out.
4 And when he leads out his flock, he goes before it and his sheep follow him, because they know his voice.
5 Now the flock will not follow a stranger, but rather it flees from him, because it does not know the voice of a stranger."

A shepherd in the East always leads the sheep and they follow his voice. This is the same idea as Psalm 23:1-2. The good shepherd will lead us to quiet waters if we follow his lead.

Mark 6:34 APNT
And Jesus disembarked [and] saw the large crowds and had compassion on them because they were like sheep that did not have a shepherd. And he began to teach them many [things].

This verse occurred right before Jesus also fed the five thousand with five loaves of bread and two fish. He was concerned about physical things as well as spiritual ones.

2. The shepherd protects the flock.

John 10:6-10 APNT
6 Jesus told them this parable, but they did not understand what he said to them.
7 Now again Jesus said to them, "Truly, truly I say to you, I am the gate of the flock.
8 And all those who come are thieves and robbers, unless the flock hears them.
9 I am the gate and if anyone should enter by me, he will live. And he will enter and he will go out and find pasture.
10 A thief does not come, except to steal and to kill and to destroy. I have come that they may have life and [that] they may have that which is abundant.

Jesus is the door of the flock. The sheepfold was an enclosure, but the door was open. The shepherd would lay in the door at night to be the protection against any predators. The picture of the rod and staff being a comfort is also important to understand at this point.

- Rod – like a policeman's club, made of wood and has a knob on the end of it. Into this knob sometimes nails are driven. It is used for protecting the sheep, fending off lions and bears.
- Staff – a stick five or six feet long and sometimes but not always has a crook at the end of it. It is used to handle the sheep and sometimes rescue them from danger, guiding them gently. It is a symbol of the shepherd's authority.

The shepherd's rod is a club used to defend himself and his sheep against predators. In *A Shepherd Looks at Psalm 23*, Phillip Keller notes another use of the rod: "Another interesting use of the rod in the shepherd's hand was to examine and count the sheep. In the terminology of the Old Testament this was referred to as passing 'under the rod': And I will cause you to pass under the rod and I will bring you into the bond of the covenant (Ezekiel 20:37). This meant not only coming under the owner's… authority, but also to be subject to his most careful, intimate and firsthand examination. A sheep that passed 'under the rod' was one which had been counted and looked over with great care. In caring for his sheep, the good shepherd… will from time to time make a careful examination of each individual sheep. As each animal comes out of the corral and through the gate, it is stopped by the shepherd's outstretched rod. He opens the fleece with the rod; he runs his skillful hands over the body; he feels for any sign of trouble; he examines the sheep with care to see that all is well. This is a most searching process entailing every intimate detail. It is, too, a comfort to the sheep for only in this way can its hidden problems be laid bare before the shepherd."[4]

The staff of the shepherd is used to gently guide the sheep in the way the shepherd wants them to go. We can pray for guidance so that we may know the way – the paths of righteousness. The staff also was used to rescue the sheep from difficult or dangerous situations, such as falling into a ditch, getting tangled in a bramble bush, or even when the wool was too heavy and the sheep fell into the water.

3. The shepherd cares for the flock and delivers it from the Evil One.

John 10:11-13 APNT
11 I am the good shepherd. A good shepherd lays down his life on behalf of his flock.

---

[4] Phillip Keller, *A Shepherd Looks at Psalm 23*, pp. 95-96.

12 But a hired servant, who is not the shepherd nor are the sheep his, when he sees a wolf coming, leaves the flock and flees. And the wolf comes [and] plunders and scatters the flock.

13 Now a hired servant flees, because he is a hired servant and he does not care about the flock.

The shepherd will protect the sheep at all costs. He will care for them in every way. The shepherd also had a sort of a "pocket" sewn into his mantle so that he could lift up an injured lamb and carry them inside the mantle next to his chest. The lamb's head would come out of one side and the feet the other. That is the picture of caring that Isaiah 40 relates.

Isaiah 40:11 KJV
He shall feed his flock like a shepherd: he shall gather the lambs with his arm, and carry them in his bosom, and shall gently lead those that are with young.

4. The shepherd knows his own and lays down his life for them.

John 10:14-18 APNT
14 I am the good shepherd and I know my own and I am known by my own,
15 as my Father knows me and I know my Father and I lay down my life on behalf of the flock.
16 Now I also have other sheep, those that are not from this sheepfold, and it is also necessary for me to bring them. And they will hear my voice and all the flock will become one and [have] one shepherd.
17 Because of this, my Father loves me, because I lay down my life that I may take it up again.

18 No one takes it away from me, but rather I lay it down by my [own] will, for I have authority to lay it down and I have authority to take it up again, for I have received this command from my Father."

The shepherd will know who is in his flock and if they have strayed or are missing, he will go and seek after them. In the end times, God will gather the lost sheep of Israel and bring them into the pasture of the Millennial Kingdom. An additional thing the shepherd does is to "feed them with justice."

Ezekiel 34:12-16 ESV
12 As a shepherd seeks out his flock when he is among his sheep that have been scattered, so will I seek out my sheep, and I will rescue them from all places where they have been scattered on a day of clouds and thick darkness.
13 And I will bring them out from the peoples and gather them from the countries, and will bring them into their own land. And I will feed them on the mountains of Israel, by the ravines, and in all the inhabited places of the country.
14 I will feed them with good pasture, and on the mountain heights of Israel shall be their grazing land. There they shall lie down in good grazing land, and on rich pasture they shall feed on the mountains of Israel.
15 I myself will be the shepherd of my sheep, and I myself will make them lie down, declares the Lord GOD.
16 I will seek the lost, and I will bring back the strayed, and I will bind up the injured, and I will strengthen the weak, and the fat and the strong I will destroy. I will feed them in justice.

When we seek the Lord in prayer for the supply of our needs, his provision relieves us of the anxiety of lack and guides us to quiet, peaceful waters. He restores and strengthens us. The simple word picture for prayer in Aramaic is **to seek the shepherding of the strong one**. When we pray in the name of Jesus the shepherd, we are invoking his care and tending.

> *1 Peter 5:10 NLT*
> *In his kindness God called you to share in his eternal glory by means of Christ Jesus. So after you have suffered a little while, he will restore, support, and strengthen you, and he will place you on a firm foundation.*

"Place you on a firm foundation" in the King James Version is to settle you. We can lie down and stop speaking about the wolves for the shepherd is our provider in every way.

ACTION ITEM: Let's think of a situation where someone needs shepherding and now quietly pray in the name of the shepherd for their deliverance!

Chapter 5 – Mediator and Advocate

In the New Testament, the term *"mediator"* is used to describe Jesus Christ and his role in reconciling men with God. The concept of a mediator involves someone who acts as a bridge or go-between, facilitating communication, reconciliation, or negotiation between two parties who are separated or in conflict. Traditionally, the Greek word *mesistos* is rendered *"mediator,"* but this conveys a wrong impression in contemporary English. Jesus was not a mediator, for example, who worked for compromise between opposing parties. In our culture, a mediator could be just a negotiator between two parties where there does not even end up being a resolution. But in the uses in the Bible, a mediator is more like an umpire or arbiter in our terminology. Once the arbiter makes a ruling or decision, it is final and binding and cannot be revoked. We call that kind of legal ruling a binding arbitration.

There are a few key passages that highlight the meaning of mediator in the New Testament.

> *1 Timothy 2:5 APNT*
> *For God is one and the mediator of God and of men is one, the man, Jesus Christ,*

Jesus was the only one able to go between man and God to enable them to have a relationship, but entirely on God's terms. Jesus is described as the mediator of the new covenant, establishing a new relationship between God and his people.

> *Hebrews 9:15 NET*
> *And so he is the mediator of a new covenant, so that those who are called may receive the eternal inheritance he has promised, since he died to set them free from the violations committed under the first covenant.*

The concept of Jesus as the mediator is rooted in the idea of sin and the separation it creates between humanity and God. The first covenant (the Law) was not able to bridge the gap between a holy God and man because of the sin nature. But when Christ paid the price for sin for everyone, all who believe on him are given an irrevocable standing and status as sons of God.

> *Hebrews 8:6 APNT*
> *And now, Jesus Christ has received a ministry that is more excellent than that, as also that covenant in which he was made the mediator is more excellent. So [it is] with the promises that are more excellent than what was given.*

The new covenant is based on better promises and provides a more profound relationship with God than the Old Testament covenant. The better promises have primarily to do with the fact that the ruling or decision is final and binding.

> *1 Timothy 2:6 NET*
> *who gave himself as a ransom for all, revealing God's purpose at his appointed time.*

Through his sacrifice, Jesus atones for the sins of humanity, bearing the punishment that sin deserves. By doing so, he provides a means for forgiveness, restoration, and reconciliation with God. Jesus' role as the mediator allows us to approach God with confidence, knowing that our sins have been forgiven and that we have been made righteous through faith in him.

The role of the law is summarized in Galatians.

Galatians 3:18-26 NLT
18 For if the inheritance could be received by keeping the law, then it would not be the result of accepting God's promise. But God graciously gave it to Abraham as a promise.
19 Why, then, was the law given? It was given alongside the promise to show people their sins. But the law was designed to last only until the coming of the child who was promised. God gave his law through angels to Moses, who was the mediator between God and the people.
20 Now a mediator is helpful if more than one party must reach an agreement. But God, who is one, did not use a mediator when he gave his promise to Abraham.
21 Is there a conflict, then, between God's law and God's promises? Absolutely not! If the law could give us new life, we could be made right with God by obeying it.
22 But the Scriptures declare that we are all prisoners of sin, so we receive God's promise of freedom only by believing in Jesus Christ.
23 Before the way of faith in Christ was available to us, we were placed under guard by the law. We were kept in protective custody, so to speak, until the way of faith was revealed.
24 Let me put it another way. The law was our guardian until Christ came; it protected us until we could be made right with God through faith.
25 And now that the way of faith has come, we no longer need the law as our guardian.
26 For you are all children of God through faith in Christ Jesus.

This concept of a mediator is found in the Old Testament in the use of the Greek word in the Septuagint in Job 9:33. The concept of a daysman fits the role of the mediator in the New Testament.

> *Job 9:33 LXX*
> *Would that he our mediator were present, and a reprover, and one who should hear the cause between both.*

> *Job 9:33 KJV*
> *Neither is there any daysman betwixt us, that might lay his hand upon us both.*

> *Job 9:33 ESV*
> *There is no arbiter between us, who might lay his hand on us both.*

The concept of the daysman comes from a Latin expression describing the fixing of a day for arbitration. Once the decision was made, the daysman laid his hand on both parties and made the ruling or decision and then it was settled.[5]

ACTION ITEM: The decision for our freedom is made final! What area of your life is in need of freedom? Imagine the daysman Jesus Christ is laying his hands on your head and making the judgment clear and final.

Jesus Christ is the mediator but he is also described as an advocate in the New Testament. An advocate is someone who speaks or acts on behalf of another, providing support, defense, or representation. In the case of Jesus, he serves as an advocate for us before God, more along the lines of a defense

---

[5] *McClintock and Strong Biblical Cyclopedia*, daysman.

45

attorney. The word in the New Testament is only used one time, but the concept is expressed in other ways.

> *1 John 2:1-2 APNT*
> *1 My sons, I am writing these [things] to you so that you do not sin. Yet if someone should sin, we have a defense attorney with the Father, Jesus Christ, the Just [one].*
> *2 For he is the payment for our sins and not on behalf of ours only, but also on behalf of [the sins of] the whole world.*

This verse highlights the role of Jesus as an advocate for us when we sin. Our carnal way of thinking fights this concept, but the spiritual reality is that Jesus has already paid for the sins of everyone in the whole world who will accept him as their Lord. Jesus advocates for us by securing forgiveness for our sins through his death on the cross. Through his atoning sacrifice, he pays the penalty for sin. His advocacy ensures that we can find forgiveness, cleansing, and restoration when we confess and repent of our sins.

> *1 John 1:8-9 APNT*
> *8 And if we say that we have no sin, we deceive ourselves and the truth is not in us.*
> *9 And if we confess our sins, he is faithful and just to forgive us our sins and to cleanse us from all our wickedness.*

> *Ephesians 1:7 APNT*
> *in whom we have redemption and remission of sins by his blood, according to the wealth of his grace,*

In the Roman culture of the Apostle Paul, one who was an "advocatus" addressed the court on behalf of his client and assisted in the conduct of a case. This was the case when Paul was a prisoner in Rome and he told Timothy, "At my first defense no one took my part, they all deserted me..." But then in the next verse he says that "the Lord stood at my side and so strengthened me." (2 Timothy 4:16-17). The Lord was his legal advisor.

Another way Jesus is our advocate is that he stands before God our Father on our behalf, interceding and providing evidence of our atonement. Jesus continually represents us, presenting our needs, prayers, and concerns before God. He understands our weaknesses and challenges, and he pleads on our behalf, offering his perfect righteousness as the basis for our acceptance before God.

> *Romans 8:34 ESV*
> *Who is to condemn? Christ Jesus is the one who died-- more than that, who was raised-- who is at the right hand of God, who indeed is interceding for us.*

Jesus provides comfort and support to us through his advocacy. Jesus understands the struggles and challenges we have in life.

> *Hebrews 4:15-16 APNT*
> *15 For we do not have a high priest who is not able to feel our weakness, but one who was tempted in everything like us, [yet] without sin.*
> *16 Therefore, we should boldly come near the throne of his grace to receive mercies and to find grace for help in time of adversity.*

In summary, Jesus is our mediator (daysman) and has made a binding ruling that we are reconciled to God as his sons. He also serves as our advocate by securing forgiveness, interceding on our behalf, and providing comfort and support.

His advocacy assures us that we can approach God with confidence, knowing that we will find mercy, grace, and help in our times of need, even in our weaknesses and failures. His role as an advocate underscores his love, care, and compassionate defense for those who trust in him.

Chapter 6 – His Name is Wonderful

In these next chapters we are going to take a look at two of Jesus' names in Isaiah 9. If you have ever heard Handel's Messiah being performed, you know that this section in Isaiah is prominent in his music. It is a very powerful and moving passage in the Word of God and tells us much about who Jesus would be. The first name we will look at is "wonderful." But let's look at the whole passage in Isaiah 9.

> *Isaiah 9:6-7 ESV*
> *6 For to us a child is born, to us a son is given; and the government shall be upon his shoulder, and his name shall be called Wonderful Counselor, Mighty God, Everlasting Father, Prince of Peace.*
> *7 Of the increase of his government and of peace there will be no end, on the throne of David and over his kingdom, to establish it and to uphold it with justice and with righteousness from this time forth and forevermore. The zeal of the LORD of hosts will do this.*

We know that now "a son is given" unto us – for our benefit – and the Messiah has come, but this verse is prophecy about his coming. The prophet saw in a vision the darkness and gloom of the nation, and saw also the son that would be born to remove that darkness and to enlighten the world. There are many verses in the New Testament such as John 3:16 about how we have been given God's son. The Messiah was to be the "gift" of God.

"Government on his shoulder" means that God has given him the same dominion as he did to Adam in the beginning. The government is represented as being carried on his shoulder. This refers to the ensign of government – the scepter, the sword, or the keys, or the like – that were suspended from it. In Isaiah 22:22 what is on his shoulder is called "the key of the house of David. "[6] The sense is that he should be a king and carry the authority of a king.

Still in Isaiah 9:6, the next phrase in the Aramaic of the Old Testament is translated "his name is called." The Hebrew is a little confusing whether it is "one calls him," implying God calls him or "he calls." The Septuagint agrees with the Aramaic Peshitta and when we put the Hebrew together with that, the one who has called him these names must be God.

The next two words of the verse usually are translated together as "wonderful counselor." Keil and Delitzsch have a great explanation of why they should be separated into two words because of the uniqueness of the Hebrew construction.[7] There is no genitive to connect the two words as the New English Translation renders it "extraordinary strategist." There are two nouns, so we will choose to separate them into two unique titles and I think when we look at both names, we can see that each has a great meaning to contribute.

Wonderful is a kind of slang word in our culture. We call all kinds of things "wonderful" – "I had a wonderful day. Always wonderful to see you. You're so wonderful." I think we might be hard-pressed to come up with a good definition for wonderful since we use it so haphazardly. But the way God uses the word "wonder" is that it is his character and who he is and what he does. It is tied in with how in the New Testament Jesus Christ is called the intercessor. We are going to be "full of wonder," to see this explanation.

---

[6] *And I will place on his shoulder the key of the house of David. He shall open, and none shall shut; and he shall shut, and none shall open. (Isaiah 22:22 ESV)*

[7] Keil and Delitzsch, *Old Testament Commentary*, Isaiah 9:6.

The Hebrew word for *"wonderful"* is *pele*. It comes from a verb, *pala*, that means *"to be marvelous, be wonderful, be surpassing, be extraordinary, separate by distinguishing action."* The noun should be translated as a wonder, marvelous thing, something extraordinary. We can see more when we look at the pictographs of the letters. The *pey* is the picture of an open mouth and means either mouth or speaking. The *lamed* is the second letter and is the shepherd's staff and means authority or guide. Putting the meanings together, *pala* means **to speak to an authority**, coming to one in authority to seek for guidance for oneself or another.

The first place *pala* occurs is when the angel tells Abraham and Sarah that the time has come for them to have a son.

> *Genesis 18:14 ESV*
> *Is anything too hard [pala] for the LORD? At the appointed time I will return to you, about this time next year, and Sarah shall have a son*

"Too hard" means extraordinary, difficult, impossible even. God caused Sarah to have a son when both of them were too old. Nothing is too difficult for God!

Jeff Benner in the *Ancient Hebrew Lexicon of the Bible* defines the pictograph of *pey and lamed* as *"a coming to one in authority to intercede on one's own behalf or for another."* He further defines a derivative root *palal* (with an additional lamed) as *"to plead for intercession or an outcome."*[8] When a letter is doubled as the *lamed* is in this verb, it can mean *"highest."* The pictograph would then mean, **to speak to the highest authority**.

---

[8] Jeff Benner, *Ancient Hebrew Lexicon of the Bible*, p. 221.

The shepherd's staff also represents guidance. In the book, *Synonyms of the Old Testament, palal* is defined as "to cause another to intervene or arbitrate in one's case... It shows that men were not in the habit of praying merely as a relief to their feelings, but in order to ask another Being, wiser and mightier than they, to take up their cause."[9] The highest authority is God, but since this is the Messiah's name, he is the one who is speaking to God as an intercessor and seeking guidance for the sheep.

Jesus is at the right hand of God and makes petition on our behalf; he is the wonderful intercessor for us.

> *Romans 8:34 ESV*
> *Who is to condemn? Christ Jesus is the one who died-- more than that, who was raised-- who is at the right hand of God, who indeed is interceding for us.*

A definition of intercessor is from the Hebrew word *paga*. One of the ways it is translated is to "strike the mark" and bring light to a situation. Job 36:32 (NIV) says, "He fills his hands with lightning and commands it to strike its mark." When God releases his light, causing it to flash from his presence like lightning, it strikes its desired target and that is likened to intercession. In Israel today, *paga* is used for "bulls-eye" in target practice. When Christ intercedes for us, it breaks the power of darkness. Spirit-led intercession helps us to hit the mark, too!

Paga can also mean "to meet." God meets with us when we pray for others. The point where two territories meet or connect is the extent to which a boundary reaches. A simple definition of intercession is to meet with God to entreat or ask

---

[9] Girdlestone, *Synonyms of the Old Testament*, p. 219.

him for something specific for another person or for yourself. We meet with God in prayer for a specific purpose. If the enemy is attacking my friend, if I want to intercede, I have to meet with God to entreat [entreat earnestly] of him an answer to help her. I am seeking for a specific answer from God to help in a specific situation. Whenever we make intercession for someone, we are meeting with God on behalf of or in place of that person.

Our intercession marks the territory as belonging to Christ. That's how we build walls of protection around others who have a need. To speak on behalf of someone else to another is a Wonder!

An important thing to see about Jesus being an intercessor for us is that he does not condemn. God cared for us so much that he sent his son to be our intercessor. That's how big God's love is for us.

> *Hebrews 7:25 APNT*
> *And he is able to give life forever to those who come near to God by way of him, for he is always alive and sends up prayer for them.*

Jesus Christ is the high priest and he has gone into the Holy of Holies to pave the way for us to have access to God. When the high priest went into the Holy of Holies on the Day of Atonement, he wore a breastplate on which were twelve stones. Each one of those stones in the breastplate represented one of the tribes of Israel. The high priest carried the names of all Israel on his chest when he went before God and it was to represent that he was standing for them on their behalf. The high priest only did that once a year and that was the only time it ever could happen. But when Jesus Christ died for us, he actually went into the Holy of Holies and sprinkled his own blood on the mercy seat. He actually carried our names with him and he fully identifies with everything in our lives.

> *Hebrews 4:14-16 APNT*
> *14 Therefore, because we have a great high priest, Jesus Christ, the Son of God, who went up to heaven, we should persist in confession of him.*
> *15 For we do not have a high priest who is not able to feel our weakness, but one who was tempted in everything like us, [yet] without sin.*
> *16 Therefore, we should boldly come near the throne of his grace to receive mercies and to find grace for help in time of adversity.*

Jesus as the intercessor carries us on his heart. There is always love involved with his petitions and with his care for us before the Father. He fully identifies with us in those things that we have need of in our life. He is a merciful and faithful high priest. Because he was a man, he lived through every single thing that we ever have to deal with. Because we have a great high priest, Jesus Christ, the son of God, who went up to heaven, we should persist in confession of him. We should be talking about how his name is wonderful. Our response to the wonder is that we should persist in declaring how great Jesus is. He's standing there doing all these wonderful things and petitioning God for us.

What is our response? We need to come boldly to the throne of grace to find help in time of need. Will you think about something that you've been going through, perhaps in just the last few days? He can identify with you about that and understands so he can intercede on your behalf and speak to God (the highest authority) to provide all the help you need.

Psalm 77:10-15 ESV
10 Then I said, "I will appeal to this, to the years of the right hand of the Most High."
11 I will remember the deeds of the LORD; yes, I will remember your wonders [pele] of old.
12 I will ponder all your work, and meditate on your mighty deeds.
13 Your way, O God, is holy. What god is great like our God?
14 You are the God who works wonders [pele]; you have made known your might among the peoples.
15 You with your arm redeemed your people, the children of Jacob and Joseph. Selah

The King James Version of verse 13 is, "Thy way, O God, is in the sanctuary." God's deeds are incomparable and set him apart as the one true God. And he has sent his Son to lead us into the sanctuary. When Jesus Christ went into the Holy of Holies, he sprinkled his blood on the mercy seat. He made the access to God's presence available and then he showed us how to go in there. Now, he actually takes us by the hand and leads us (guidance) to be able to understand how to have communion with God every day. He knows the path, right? He knows the way to have fellowship and communion with God the Father.

Psalm 107:8 ESV
Let them thank the LORD for his steadfast love, for his wondrous works [pele] to the children of man!

There are four times in this psalm this verse is repeated. Jesus' name is wonderful, and it is because of God's steadfast love and loving-kindness. Jesus Christ now acts as our high priest and intercedes on our behalf and guides us into communion with God our Father.

Hebrews 10:19-23 APNT
19 We have, therefore, my brothers, boldness in the entering of the sanctuary by the blood of Jesus
20 and a way of life that is now made new for us by the veil that is his flesh.
21 And we have a high priest over the house of God.
22 Therefore, we should come near with a steadfast heart and with the confidence of faith, our hearts being sprinkled and pure from an evil conscience and our body washed with pure water.
23 And we should persist in the confession of our hope and we should not waver, for he is faithful who promised us.

Let's persist in the confession of our hope because Jesus Christ is Wonderful!

An example of how to pray like this is found in Psalm 57 when David fled from Saul in the cave.

Psalm 57:1-3 NLT
1 Have mercy on me, O God, have mercy! I look to you for protection. I will hide beneath the shadow of your wings until the danger passes by.
2 I cry out to God Most High, to God who will fulfill his purpose for me.
3 He will send help from heaven to rescue me, disgracing those who hound me. Interlude. My God will send forth his unfailing love and faithfulness.

ACTION ITEM: Make intercession for someone who has a need and picture the light of God's presence and Jesus Christ's intercession clearing away the darkness like lightning dropping on the spot!

Chapter 7 – Counselor

"The government shall be upon his shoulder and his name is to be called wonderful," and then counselor. We will be looking at what this title means, but also what is the relationship to the New Testament and what we know about Jesus Christ, what he accomplished and what he does today.

The Hebrew word for counsel is *ya'atz* and is defined as "to advise, consult, give counsel, purpose or devise a plan." The word picture is formed of three letters, *yud*, *ayin*, and *tsade*. The *yud* is a pictograph of a hand and means power or work. The *ayin* is the picture of an eye and means to see or experience. The *tsade* is the picture of a man on his side and means to follow the trail or seek. Putting those three letters together, counsel means **the power to see how to follow the trail**. In order to follow the trail, we need counsel or advice.

In Frank Seekins' book on the Hebrew word pictures, he says it is *"the hand that knows the hook."* He takes the *tsade* to be hook. This actually contributes a little more to our understanding when we look at how a counselor counsels. A person who counsels knows the pitfalls of the trail, where the snakes are, how to go around the rocks.[10]

Jeff Benner defines the pictograph as *"the upright and firmness of a tree."*[11] He adds the *yud* to the word for tree, *'etz*. In the Eastern culture, the elders were considered the pillars of the community, like trees, and were the ones that you came to for advice and for counsel. One could put all these definitions together to mean, **the power or firmness of how to follow the trail experienced**.

---

[10] Frank Seekins, *Hebrew Word Pictures*, p. 157.
[11] Jeff Benner, *Ancient Hebrew Lexicon of the Bible*, p. 215.

When we go back to Isaiah 9 and see verse 7, we read of the zeal of the Lord of Hosts who will bring to pass the reign of this king who will be a counselor and will reign with justice.

Isaiah 9:7 ESV
Of the increase of his government and of peace there will be no end, on the throne of David and over his kingdom, to establish it and to uphold it with justice and with righteousness from this time forth and forevermore. The zeal of the LORD of hosts will do this.

Later in Isaiah, he gets the vision of how the Messiah will be a branch and will give counsel with great wisdom.

Isaiah 11:1-5 ESV
1 There shall come forth a shoot from the stump of Jesse, and a branch from his roots shall bear fruit.
2 And the Spirit of the LORD shall rest upon him, the Spirit of wisdom and understanding, the Spirit of counsel [etzah] and might, the Spirit of knowledge and the fear of the LORD.
3 And his delight shall be in the fear of the LORD. He shall not judge by what his eyes see, or decide disputes by what his ears hear,
4 but with righteousness he shall judge the poor, and decide with equity for the meek of the earth; and he shall strike the earth with the rod of his mouth, and with the breath of his lips he shall kill the wicked.
5 Righteousness shall be the belt of his waist, and faithfulness the belt of his loins.

The Messiah will not judge by what his eyes see or by what his ears hear. He is not going to walk by sight or by his own senses, but with righteousness he will judge the poor or meek. The part about the rod of his mouth is at the end times when he comes back as King of kings and Lord of lords. Later in verse 10, there is another description of an event in the end times.

> *Isaiah 11:10 ESV*
> *In that day the root of Jesse, who shall stand as a signal for the peoples-- of him shall the nations inquire, and his resting place shall be glorious.*

The name of the Messiah is counselor because he is the one who fulfilled and will fulfill every part of God's plan. He will be the one that will defeat the Antichrist (who in the following verse is called the Assyrian) eventually. The power to see how to follow a trail is all wrapped up with God's purposes and counsel that he planned from the foundation of the world. And God is not going to let anything stop his plans from happening.

> *Isaiah 14:24-27 ESV*
> *24 The LORD of hosts has sworn: "As I have planned, so shall it be, and as I have purposed [ya'atz], so shall it stand,*
> *25 that I will break the Assyrian in my land, and on my mountains trample him underfoot; and his yoke shall depart from them, and his burden from their shoulder."*
> *26 This is the purpose [etzah] that is purposed [ya'atz] concerning the whole earth, and this is the hand that is stretched out over all the nations.*
> *27 For the LORD of hosts has purposed [ya'atz], and who will annul it? His hand is stretched out, and who will turn it back?*

Isaiah further explains that when God speaks, He brings his Word to pass.

Isaiah 46:9-10 ESV
9 remember the former things of old; for I am God, and
there is no other; I am God, and there is none like me,
10 declaring the end from the beginning and from ancient
times things not yet done, saying, 'My counsel [etzah]
shall stand, and I will accomplish all my purpose,'

The counsel of the Lord will always stand because he knows
the end from the beginning. He knew that he would send his
Son to fulfill the redemption for mankind.

Psalm 33:9-11 ESV
9 For he spoke, and it came to be; he commanded, and it
stood firm.
10 The LORD brings the counsel [etzah] of the nations to
nothing; he frustrates the plans of the peoples.
11 The counsel [etzah] of the LORD stands forever, the
plans of his heart to all generations.

Not only is the Messiah a counselor par excellence, but God
has given us the mind of Christ as our counselor.

1 Corinthians 2:16 NET
For who has known the mind of the Lord, so as to advise
him? But we have the mind of Christ.

This is a quotation of a passage in Isaiah 40.

Isaiah 40:13-14 ESV
13 Who has measured the Spirit of the LORD, or what
man shows him his counsel [etzah]?
14 Whom did he consult [ya'atz], and who made him
understand? Who taught him the path of justice, and
taught him knowledge, and showed him the way of
understanding?

In conclusion, not only did God know he would send the Messiah and fulfill his plans of redemption for man, but he hid the mystery of the one body in his heart that one day in the administration of the fulness of times, he would gather together all things in Christ. It was God's foreknowledge that the Messiah would come and he would be the epitome of the counselor in bringing God's will to pass.

> *Ephesians 1:9-12 APNT*
> *9 And he made known to us the mystery of his will that he had determined beforehand to accomplish in him,*
> *10 in the administration of the fullness of times, that everything that is in heaven and in earth should be made new again in Christ.*
> *11 And we were chosen in him, even as he marked us out beforehand and he desired, he who performs everything according to the purpose of his will,*
> *12 that we, those who first trusted in Christ, should be for the esteem of his magnificence.*

We have the mind of Christ by way of the gift of the Holy Spirit. That Spirit is one of mighty counsel and gives us the power to see how to follow the trail of God's plans.

ACTION ITEM: Spend some time with God and ask him to show you what his plans are for you, who your team is and what his mission is for you in the immediate future.

Chapter 8 – Jesus the Prophet

We have seen so far that Jesus was anointed as the High Priest, as the Intercessor and as a King just like the people in the Old Testament. He was also anointed as a prophet. In this chapter we will investigate how he was THE prophet.

Moses foreshadows what Jesus Christ would be as a prophet. He was the mouthpiece of God, calling people to repentance and teaching them about the coming of the Messiah. In the unfolding of the Law, all the offerings, the tabernacle itself and the feasts all point to Christ and are fulfilled in him.

It was revealed to Moses that the Messiah would be a greater prophet than even Moses, who received great revelation. Moses was a prophet in two ways: by his actions and through his words. Some of his actions were delivering Israel from Egypt, performing great signs and wonders (including passing through the Red Sea) and leading the people in battle against their enemies. His words included the teaching of the meaning of redemption on the night of Passover, and the first five books of the Bible are the explanation of the Law and how to live it.

> *Deuteronomy 18:18 ESV*
> *I will raise up for them a prophet like you from among their brothers. And I will put my words in his mouth, and he shall speak to them all that I command him.*

This prophecy was fulfilled in Jesus' ministry. In Hebrews, it also says that Jesus was to be a greater prophet than Moses. How was he greater?

1. He was a greater builder (Hebrews 3:1-6).

Hebrews 3:3 APNT
For the glory of this [man] is much greater than that of Moses, just as the honor of the builder of the house [is] much greater than [that of] his building.

2. There was a greater exodus (from sin).

Hebrews 2:17 APNT
Because of this, it is right that he should be made like his brothers in everything, so that he would be a merciful and faithful high priest in the things of God and would make atonement for the sins of the people.

3. There is a greater promised land (life in the age to come).

Hebrews 5:8-9 APNT
8 And although he was a Son, from the fear and the sufferings that he bore, he learned obedience.
9 And so he was matured and became for all those who obey him the cause of eternal life.

Luke 7:16 APNT (after raising the son who died in village of Nain)
And fear took hold of all men and they were praising God and saying, "A great prophet has risen up among us and God has visited his people."

CHARACTERISTICS OF JESUS AS A PROPHET

- Jesus revealed the heart of God as a Father.

John 5:17-21 APNT
17 But Jesus said to them, "My Father works until now. I also work."

18 And because of this, the Judeans were seeking to kill him even more, not only because he had broken the Sabbath, but also because he was saying about God that he was his Father and was equating himself with God.

19 Now Jesus answered and said to them, "Truly, truly I say to you, the Son is not able to do anything by his own will, but what he sees the Father [do], that he does. For those [things] that the Father does, these also the Son does likewise.

20 For the Father loves his Son and everything that he does, he shows him and he will show him greater than these works, so that you will marvel.

21 For as the Father raises the dead and makes them alive, so also the Son will make alive those whom he wants.

- Jesus warned and corrected the Pharisees but also the people. An example is in the Sermon on the Mount.

Matthew 5:17 APNT
Do not think that I have come to change the law or the prophets. I have not come to change, but to fulfill [them].

Starting in verse 21, Jesus says a number of times, "You have heard that it was said…but I say to you…"

Matthew 5:21-22 APNT
21 You have heard that it was said to the ancient [ones]: YOU SHOULD NOT KILL. And ANYONE WHO KILLS IS CONDEMNED TO JUDGMENT.
22 But I say to you, whoever provokes his brother to anger without cause is condemned to judgment. And anyone who says to his brother, '[I] spit [on you]!' is

condemned to the assembly. And he, who says, 'Fool,' is condemned to the Gehenna of fire.

Matthew 5:43-44 APNT
43 You have heard that it was said: LOVE YOUR NEIGHBOR AND HATE YOUR ENEMY.
44 But I say to you, love your enemies and bless those who curse you and do that which is pleasing to him who hates you and pray for those who take you by force and persecute you,

- He was a "justice warrior."

Acts 10:38 ESV
how God anointed Jesus of Nazareth with the Holy Spirit and with power. He went about doing good and healing all who were oppressed by the devil, for God was with him.

SOME EXAMPLES OF PROPHECIES JESUS GAVE

1. He gave prophecies about himself, including that he would be rejected, executed and resurrected.

   Matthew 12:38-40 APNT
   38 Then answered some of the scribes and of the Pharisees and said to him, "Teacher, we desire to see a sign from you."
   39 But he answered and said to them, "An evil and adulterous generation seeks a sign, yet a sign will not be given to it, except the sign of Jonah the prophet.
   40 For as Jonah was in the belly of the fish three days and three nights, so will the Son of Man be in the heart of the earth three days and three nights.

Luke 24:44-49 APNT
44 And he said to them, "These are the words that I spoke to you while I was with you, that it was necessary that everything be fulfilled that was written in the law of Moses and in the prophets and in the Psalms about me."
45 Then he opened their minds to understand the scriptures.
46 And he said to them, "So it is written and so it was right that the Messiah should suffer and rise from the dead after three days
47 and that repentance will be preached through his name for the forgiveness of sins in all the nations and [that] the beginning will be from Jerusalem.
48 And you are a witness of these [things]
49 and I will send to you the promise of my Father. But remain in the city, Jerusalem, until you be clothed with power from on high."

2. He gave prophecies about his followers including that they would desert him, betray him and deny him, and also that they would be successful in preaching the gospel to the world.

Matthew 26:21 APNT
"...one of you will betray me."

Matthew 26:31 NIV
"...This very night you will all fall away on account of me..."

Luke 22:34 NASB
"...the rooster will not crow today until you have denied three times that you know Me."

John 1:45-51 APNT
45 And Philip found Nathaniel and said to him, "We have found him about whom Moses wrote in the law and the prophets, that he is Jesus the son of Joseph from Nazareth."
46 Nathaniel said to him, "Is it possible for anything good to be from Nazareth?" Philip said to him, "Come and you will see."
47 And Jesus saw Nathaniel coming towards him and said about him, "Behold, truly a son of Israel in whom there is no deceit."
48 Nathaniel said to him, "From where do you know me?" Jesus said to him, "Before Philip called you, while you were under the fig tree, I saw you."
49 Nathaniel answered and said to him, "My Master, you are the Son of God. You are the King of Israel."
50 Jesus said to him, "Because I told you that I saw you under the fig tree, do you believe? For you will see greater [things] than these."
51 He said to him, "Truly, truly I say to you, from now on you will see heaven opening and the angels of God ascending and descending to the Son of Man."

Acts 1:4-8 APNT
4 And as he ate bread with them, he commanded them that they should not leave Jerusalem, but that they should wait for the promise of the Father, about which [he said], "You have heard from me.
5 For John baptized with water, yet you will be baptized with the Holy Spirit after not many days."
6 Now while they were assembled, they asked him and said to him, "Our Lord, at this time will you restore the kingdom to Israel?"

7 He said to them, "This is not yours to know the time or these times that the Father has placed in his own authority.
8 But when the Holy Spirit comes on you, you will receive power and you will be witnesses for me in Jerusalem and in all Judea and also among the Samaritans, even to the ends of the earth."

3. He gave prophecies about Israel, that the temple would be destroyed.

Luke 19:41-44 APNT (after the triumphal entry)
41 And when he came near and saw the city, he wept over it.
42 And he said, "Would that you had known those [things] that were for your peace, even in this your day, but now they are hidden from your eyes.
43 But the days will come to you when your enemies will surround you and will pressure you on every side.
44 And they will overthrow you and your children within you and they will not leave a stone on a stone in you, for you did not know the time of your visitation."

Matthew 24:1-2 APNT
1 And Jesus came out of the temple to go away. And his disciples came near [and] were showing him the construction of the temple.
2 And he said to them, "Behold, do you not see all these [things]? Truly I say to you, [one] stone here will not be left on [another] stone that will not be demolished."

4. He gave prophecies about the future and his return to set up his kingdom.

Matthew 24:3-8 APNT
3 And when Jesus sat on the Mount of Olives, his disciples came near and said among themselves and to him, "Tell us when these [things] will be and what is the sign of your coming and of the end of the age."
4 Jesus answered and said to them, "Beware, [so that] no one will deceive you.
5 For many will come in my name and they will say, 'I am the Messiah.' And they will deceive many.
6 Now you are about to hear of battles and a report of wars. See [that] you are not disturbed. For it is necessary that all these [things] occur, but the end [is] not yet.
7 For people will rise against people and kingdom against kingdom and famines and pestilence and earthquakes will occur in various places.
8 But all these [things] are [only] the beginning of sorrows.

5. He gave prophecies about the Comforter to come.

John 14:26 APNT
But that Deliverer, the Holy Spirit, whom my Father will send in my name, will teach you everything and will remind you of all that I said to you.

See also John 14:16, 15:26 and 16:7.

A prophet is one who sees the future and also the heart of a person. Jesus was the greatest prophet so when we want to know what the Father's heart is or what will come to pass, or a vision for our lives, go to Jesus the prophet and seek his wisdom and perspective. He will not withhold any good thing from us.

JESUS THE PROPHET

Luke 21:33 APNT
Heaven and earth will pass away, yet my words will not pass away.

ACTION ITEM: Get a pen. Ask the Lord to reveal his heart for you and how much he loves you. Write down what words come to mind.

Chapter 9 – The Prince of Peace

There are a number of different ways to translate some of the titles in Isaiah 9:6. We have discussed a few of them already concerning "wonderful" and "counselor." Here is the Septuagint version of this verse.

> *Isaiah 9:6 LXX*
> *For a child is born to us, and a son is given to us, whose government is upon his shoulder: and his name is called the Messenger of great counsel: for I will bring peace upon the princes, and health to him.*

The Peshitta Old Testament translates the phrase, "the mighty God" as "the mighty man of eternity."

> *Isaiah 9:6 Peshitta Holy Bible Translated*
> *Because the Child is born to us, and the Son is given to us, and his authority was on his shoulder, and his Name was called The Wonder and The Counselor, God, the Mighty Man of Eternity, the Prince of Peace [and The Father of Eternity]*

I have worked on a further translation of the Syriac as follows:

…he will be called Wonder (a Marvel and Intercessor) and Counselor (Advisor), Mighty Hero (Champion) of the ages, Ruler (Captain) of Peace and Father (Originator) of the age that is prepared to come.

For more discussion of "mighty hero" please read Chapter 11 on the Breaker. This chapter will focus on the Ruler of Peace.

The Hebrew is *Sar Shalom*. *Sar* can mean prince, ruler, leader, chief, chieftain, official, captain, leader, general, commander (military), or overseer. In *Barnes' Notes on the Bible* of this passage, he describes the phrase "prince of peace" as follows:

> This is a Hebrew mode of expression denoting that he would be a peaceful prince. The tendency of his administration would be to restore and perpetuate peace. This expression is used to distinguish him from the mass of kings and princes who have delighted in conquest and blood. In contradistinction from all these, the Messiah would seek to promote universal concord, and the tendency of his reign would be to put an end to wars, and to restore harmony and order to the nations.[12]

The Targum of Jonathan renders it: "The Messiah, whose peace shall be multiplied upon us in his days." People will be able to "lie down in safety."

> *Hosea 2:18 NLT*
> *On that day I will make a covenant with all the wild animals and the birds of the sky and the animals that scurry along the ground so they will not harm you. I will remove all weapons of war from the land, all swords and bows, so you can live unafraid in peace and safety.*

Shalom has the idea of completeness in it, not only the absence of strife. Jesus is called the Prince of Peace because he is the author of peace today as well as in the future. He made peace between the Jew and Gentile. By the blood of the cross, having the chastisement of their peace laid on him, he was able to reconcile the world to God.

---

[12] Albert Barnes, *Barnes' Notes on the Bible*, Isaiah 9:6.

Ephesians 2:13-18 ESV
13 But now in Christ Jesus you who once were far off
have been brought near by the blood of Christ.
14 For he himself is our peace, who has made us both one
and has broken down in his flesh the dividing wall of
hostility
15 by abolishing the law of commandments expressed in
ordinances, that he might create in himself one new man
in place of the two, so making peace,
16 and might reconcile us both to God in one body
through the cross, thereby killing the hostility.
17 And he came and preached peace to you who were far
off and peace to those who were near.
18 For through him we both have access in one Spirit to
the Father.

There are many places in the New Testament that talk of the
peace that Jesus Christ has brought to us as sons of God. "We
have peace with God through our Lord Jesus Christ" (Romans
5:1), the kingdom of God is "peace and joy in the Holy Spirit"
(Romans 14:17). Peace is also a fruit of the Spirit (Galatians
5:22) and we have "unity of the Spirit in the bond of peace"
(Ephesians 4:3). Peace can "guard our heart and minds"
(Philippians 4:7) and we have "peace at all times and in every
way" (2 Thessalonians 3:16). These are just a few ways we
have peace now.

Another name of Jesus which is similar to "Prince of Peace"
is Shiloh and it is in the prophecy of Jacob over Judah.

Genesis 49:10 KJV
The sceptre shall not depart from Judah, nor a lawgiver
from between his feet, until Shiloh come; and unto him
shall the gathering of the people be.

This is the only place with this exact spelling of the Hebrew word so there has been much speculation about what it means. With different vowels, it can mean "to whom it belongs."

Genesis 49:10 NET
The scepter will not depart from Judah, nor the ruler's staff from between his feet, until he comes to whom it belongs; the nations will obey him.

I read a sermon that Charles Spurgeon did in 1894 and he had a very different understanding.[13] Shiloh comes from the root verb *shalah* which means to rest, prosper, be quiet. Thus, the name Shiloh is rest-giver, quiet-giver, rest-maker. He will be the rest-maker when he ushers in the Millennial kingdom, the sabbath rest of 1000 years for Israel. See how it is similar to "Prince of Peace?" And Jesus is a rest-maker now, too.

This interpretation can be confirmed in the companion word in Aramaic, *shela*. It is used when there was a great storm on the sea of Galilee and Jesus was asleep in the back of the boat and the disciples were all upset, "Teacher, do you not care that we are perishing?"

Mark 4:39 APNT
And he rose up and rebuked the wind and said to the sea, "Cease [shela]; be restrained." And the wind ceased [shela] and a great calm [quiet] occurred.

Shalah causes dramatic change in the spiritual climate of situations by having something negative cease. Hence, there is peace that replaces the storm.

---

[13] https://www.spurgeon.org/resource-library/sermons/shiloh/#flipbook/

Now that we know about these names, let us see the application today. 2 Corinthians 10:4 says "the weapons of our warfare are not carnal..." The word picture for weapon is **implement in our hand**. One of our weapons is the name of Jesus Christ.

> *John 14:13 APNT*
> *And whatever you ask in my name, I will do for you, so that the Father will be glorified by his Son.*

If someone is in need of peace, rest and a dramatic change, we can pray in the name of the Prince of Peace and Shiloh. Then he will go to work to cause the storm to cease as the ruler of peace, the rest-maker and rest-giver.

ACTION ITEM: Consider the anointing you have in Christ. Stand in the gap for someone who needs rest today and command the storm, with a peaceful confidence, to cease in the name of the Ruler of Peace.

Chapter 10 – The Captain of Salvation

The names and titles of Jesus Christ show not only what he has accomplished but also what he is doing today. Seated at right hand of God means he has all authority, but also that he is carrying out God's will as his CEO (chief executive officer). He has given us his name to use in our prayer life and that name is above every other name.

Captain is the Greek work *archegos*, from *archo*, to be first, rule, take commencement. The Aramaic word is *risha*. *Archegos* is translated prince, captain and author in the King James Version. One definition is "one that takes the lead in anything and thus affords an example, a predecessor in a matter, pioneer."[14]

The first use of *archegos* and *risha* is in Acts 3 right after the man at gate Beautiful was healed.

> *Acts 3:12-16 APNT*
> *12 And when Simon saw [it], he answered and said to them, "Men, sons of Israel, why do you wonder at this [man]? Or why do you look at us as if by our own power or by our authority we did this, so that this [man] would walk?*
> *13 The God of Abraham and of Isaac and of Jacob, the God of our fathers, has glorified his Son Jesus, whom you delivered up and denied in the presence of Pilate, after he had thought it right to let him go.*
> *14 But you denied the Holy and Just [one] and requested that a murderer should be given to you.*
> *15 And you killed that Prince [risha] of Life, whom God raised from the dead. And we all are his witnesses.*

---

[14] *Thayer's Greek-English Lexicon of the New Testament*, archegos.

16 And by the faith of his name he has strengthened and healed this [man], whom you see and know, and faith that is in him has given him this wholeness before all of you.

Jesus is the first or predecessor of all who will be raised from the dead. Some translations call him "the author of life." By his name the man was healed who had been unable to walk since birth. No wonder people were astounded at this miracle!

The second use of the word for "captain" is in Acts 5.

Acts 5:29-32 APNT
29 Simon answered with the apostles and said to them, "It is right to be persuaded by God, more than by men.
30 The God of our fathers raised Jesus, whom you killed when you hung him on the tree.
31 God has established this [man as] a leader [risha] and savior and has elevated him by his right hand to give repentance and forgiveness of sins to Israel.
32 And we are witnesses of these words and [so] is the Holy Spirit that God gives to those who believe in him."

Archegos is translated in this verse as a leader and then immediately ties that in with the word for savior. You could put these two titles together as the figure of speech, *hendiadys*: a saving leader, or a saving captain. The word savior in Aramaic means "life-giver." This is what Jesus is doing now. He is leading and being the predecessor of all things. And he's also giving life to us in every way that we need it.

Archegos is also used 35 times in the Septuagint as captain or a military leader. A captain leads the way to capture new territory.

Judges 11:6 KJV
And they said unto Jephthah, Come, and be our captain
[archegos], that we may fight with the children of
Ammon.

Friberg's *Analytical Lexicon to the Greek New Testament* has
the following definition of *archegos* that combines the idea of
pioneer with a founder: *"*(1) strictly *one who goes first on the*
path; hence *leader, prince, pioneer*; (2) as one who causes
something to begin *originator, founder, initiator. "*

Hebrews 12:1-2 APNT
1 Because of this also, we, who have all these witnesses
that surround us like a cloud, should unfasten all our
burdens from us, even the sin that is always prepared for
us, and we should run with patience this race that is set
for us.
2 And we should look at Jesus, who was the initiator
[risha] and finisher of our faith, who for the joy there was
for him endured the cross and discounted the shame and
sat down at the right hand of the throne of God.

The King James Version says: "Looking unto Jesus the author
and finisher of *our* faith; who for the joy that was set before
him endured the cross, despising the shame, and is set down
at the right hand of the throne of God. " Set down means that
it was finished. It was completed. There was no more work to
do once he had endured the cross. God raised him from the
dead and after that, he spent forty days on the earth showing
his resurrected body and then he ascended into heaven. The
work is finished. That's why it calls him the finisher of our
faith, too.

The New English Translation notes on this verse are
interesting: "The Greek word translated *pioneer* is used of a

"prince" or leader, the representative head of a family. It also carries nuances of "trailblazer," one who breaks through to new ground for those who follow him."

So now let's put together some of the definitions we have learned so far in this verse. He is the pioneer, the founder, the predecessor, the one who started it all. He is also the finisher of faith because he had the full measure of faith and he had a full measure of Holy Spirit. He has now given that to us to use. We should look at that. We should look at Jesus and trust that he is still leading the way to capture new territory. He's still the trailblazer. He's still the one who breaks through new ground so we can follow him. And we can also use his name as this leader and pioneer in our prayers and we can rely upon his faith. In the past, I think that I was stuck with the idea that I had to have all this faith or I had to grow up in faith, but the truth is that we have all of Christ's faith. It just needs to be energized. We already have it. Because Jesus had the full measure of faith, he has now given that to us to use as part of our gift.

The last section of scripture in the New Testament further explains how Jesus is our captain.

> *Hebrews 2:5-6 APNT*
> *5 For he did not subject the age that is to come, about which we speak, to angels.*
> *6 But as the scripture witnesses and says: WHAT IS MAN THAT YOU REMEMBER HIM AND THE SON OF MAN THAT YOU VISIT HIM?*

"The age that is to come" is referring to the coming kingdom when Jesus Christ is reigning. God didn't subject that age to angels. So that's important to note there. But as the scripture witnesses and says in verse 6, "What is man that you

THE CAPTAIN OF SALVATION

remember him and the son of man that you visit him?" This starts a quotation from Psalm 8. And this is a kind of question, *erotesis*, that should cause us to ponder what the answer is. Well, what is man? What should I think about man? Jesus was a man and he is called the Son of Man. He had physical things that he had to do every day and he was a man with human feelings. So, what about man versus angels? God, why did you pick a man to be the savior, the deliverer?

> *Hebrews 2:7-8a APNT*
> *7 You humbled him lower than the angels. You placed on his head glory and honor and gave him authority over the work of your hands*
> *8 and you subjected everything under his feet...*

This section is a quotation of Psalm 8:4-6. "...a little lower than the Elohim" is interpreted correctly by Paul as angels. The word "little" is either in measure or time, so it is possible to translate this as "lower than the angels for a little while" as in the New English Translation. That really clears up the whole idea of why he was humbled lower than the angels. That was for the period of time when he was on the earth. But now that he is the resurrected Christ, the Lord seated at the right hand of God, he has all authority over all the work of God's hands.

> *Hebrews 2:8b-10 APNT*
> *8 ...Now in that he subjected everything to him, he did not leave out anything that was not subjected. But now, we do not yet see that everything is subjected to him.*
> *9 But we see him, who was humbled lower than the angels, to be [this] Jesus, because of the suffering of his death. And glory and honor are placed on his head, for by the grace of God, he tasted death in place of everyone.*

10 For it was proper for him, by whose hand everything [was] and for whose sake everything [was] and [who] brought many sons into glory, that he should perfect the prince of their life by his suffering.

Jesus is the man who fulfilled Psalm 8 by suffering death and then being exalted to God's right hand. He had to share in our humanity, to suffer and to die, so that we might share in his glory. He is the author or pioneer of salvation – he's the trailblazer for the saving of many, many sons who are going to join him in the age to come, reigning over all of God's creation. We get to have that privilege. We're the many sons and we will then also be above the angels. At that point we get to share completely in Jesus Christ's glory and honor. Oh, if we could just get that into our hearts!

Hebrews 2:11-18 APNT
11 For he who makes holy and those who are made holy are all of one. Because of this, he is not ashamed to call them his brothers,
12 saying: I WILL ANNOUNCE YOUR NAME TO MY BROTHERS AND I WILL PRAISE YOU WITHIN THE CHURCH.
13 And again: I WILL BE CONFIDENT ABOUT HIM, and again, BEHOLD, I AND THE CHILDREN THAT GOD HAS GIVEN ME.
14 For because the sons share in flesh and blood, he also in the same manner shared of the same, that by his death he would put a stop to him who held the authority of death, who is Satan,
15 and would release those who by fear of death were subjected to bondage all their lives.
16 For he did not assume [a nature] from the angels, but he assumed death from the seed of Abraham.

17 Because of this, it is right that he should be made like his brothers in everything, so that he would be a merciful and faithful high priest in the things of God and would make atonement for the sins of the people.
18 For in that which he [himself] suffered and was tempted, he is able to help those who are tempted.

Jesus shared of the same humanity as us, so that by his death, he would put a stop to him who held the authority of death, who is Satan, and would release those who by fear of death were subjected to bondage all their lives. That's what Jesus Christ did for us – he released us from the fear of death and the bondage because of that. Verse 16 explains that he did not assume a nature of an angel, but he assumed death from the seed of Abraham. It is right that he should be made like his brothers [us] in everything so that he would be a merciful and faithful high priest in the things of God. He is able to help those who are tempted. So that's another thing that Jesus is doing right now. He is the trailblazer to lead us out and to help all those who are being tempted still today and who have fear of death and who are in bondage. He's the predecessor, he's our captain, he's our military leader.

Jesus is now not only our captain but the head of the Body. Captain is the word *risha* in Aramaic and it also means head, or first leader.

Ephesians 1:19-23 KJV
19 And what is the exceeding greatness of his power to us-ward who believe, according to the working of his mighty power,
20 Which he wrought in Christ, when he raised him from the dead, and set him at his own right hand in the heavenly places,

21 Far above all principality, and power, and might, and dominion, and every name that is named, not only in this world, but also in that which is to come:
22 And hath put all things under his feet, and gave him to be the head [risha] over all things to the church,
23 Which is his body, the fulness of him that filleth all in all.

Jesus has the highest name of all! He has given us the right to use his name and all things will be put under our feet, too, in the future. So now substitute the word head for captain, trailblazer, pioneer, predecessor. Jesus is the head over all things to the church, not only just the guide, but the captain. If you have a captain in an army and you're going to go fight a battle, you follow the captain and listen to him. You're going to say, "Sir, what are the orders today?" And we can do that with the same idea of Jesus Christ being the head of the body.

We have the full measure of Holy Spirit that Christ had. We have the full measure of faith. We have the authority to use his name to get answers to prayer. There's no room then for discouragement or despair because we have such a great hope. The work is done in Christ. Christ is the second Adam. He will reign and rule in the age to come. But we are going to rule with him, all his brothers, all the ones that the captain of salvation brought to God, we are going to live and reign with him and be partakers of His salvation forever. Jesus is the captain of salvation. We need to grow up into Him.

Ephesians 4:14-16 APNT
14 And we should not be babies, who are shaken and blown about by every wind of the deceitful teachings of men, who in their craftiness are plotting to deceive.
15 But we should be steadfast in our love, so that [in] everything we ourselves may grow up in Christ, who is

the head [captain, ruler, prince, author and finisher of our salvation].
16 And from him the whole body is fit together and is knit together in all the joints, according to the gift that is given by measure to each member for the growth of the body, that its building up would be accomplished in love.

ACTION ITEM: Ask the Lord
What is your assignment for me today? Where is the trail?

Chapter 11 – The Breaker

We have seen in previous chapters that Jesus is Lord, meaning he is Master and he is the greatest Lord. When he returns, he will be coming as King of kings and Lord of lords. One of the first things he will do (and we will be with him) is to go and rescue the Jews who are hiding in the desert in Bozrah. He will break them out of the gate and lead them. His name is *Peretz*, the Breaker.

> *Micah 2:12-13 KJV*
> *12 I will surely assemble, O Jacob, all of thee; I will surely gather the remnant of Israel; I will put them together as the sheep of Bozrah, as the flock in the midst of their fold: they shall make great noise by reason of the multitude of men.*
> *13 The breaker is come up before them: they have broken up, and have passed through the gate, and are gone out by it: and their king shall pass before them, and the LORD on the head of them.*

In this verse, the term "breaker" is used metaphorically to describe a leader or a victorious figure who goes ahead of the people, breaking through obstacles or barriers. It portrays a dynamic and powerful image of someone who leads a group, paving the way for them to move forward and overcome hindrances.

The root verb for breaker is *peretz* and means to break through, break down, break into, break open. The verb is used some fifty times in the Old Testament, often in a military or disaster situation. The subject may be God or man. When God is the subject, it describes his activity against an enemy. Speaking of an attack against the Philistines, David said the Lord helped him to break through.

2 Samuel 5:20 ESV
And David came to Baal-perazim, and David defeated
them there. And he said, "The LORD has broken through
my enemies before me like a breaking flood." Therefore
the name of that place is called Baal-perazim.

Jesus as the Breaker breaks through the enemy that has them in prison. Then he enlarges the gate so all can pass through, leading with the LORD Jehovah at the head (the two of them together).

Micah 2:13 NET
The one who can break through barriers will lead them
out they will break out, pass through the gate, and leave.
Their king will advance before them, The LORD himself
will lead them.

In the context of Micah's prophecy, this verse speaks of God's deliverance and restoration of his people. It depicts a leader or king who leads the people out of captivity, breaking through the gates of oppression or exile, and leading them to freedom. The image emphasizes God's active role in the redemption and liberation of his people, with the Lord himself going before them as their ultimate leader and guide.

In *Witness of the Stars*, Bullinger identifies the etymology of the word Perseus to be related to the word for "breaker." Perseus is the constellation just above Taurus and its traditional illustration is a warrior that has cut off the head of Satan or the gorgon Medusa. In Greek mythology, he rescues the maiden Andromeda from a sea monster. Here is an excerpt from Bullinger's description:

This is what is pictured to us here. We see a glorious "Breaker" taking His place before His redeemed, breaking forth at their head, breaking down all barriers, and breaking the heads of Leviathan and all his hosts. In His right hand He has His "sore, and great, and strong sword" lifted up to smite and break down the enemy. He has wings on His feet, which tells us that He is coming very swiftly. In His left hand He carries the head of the enemy, who he has slain.[15]

Some of the constellation's names for Perseus are "the Champion," "the Hero," and "the Rescuer."[16] This reminds me of Martin Luther's translation of "Mighty Hero" in Isaiah 9:6. Some of the meanings of the stars in the constellation are: Al Genib – one who steals away suddenly, Atik – to burst bonds asunder, Rosh Satan (Al Gol) – the head of Satan. The name of Medusa comes from a Hebrew word *shuwph* and is used in Genesis 3:15 about the promised seed who would "bruise" the head of the serpent.[17]

---

[15] E.W. Bullinger, *Witness of the Stars*, p. 115.
[16] Richard Allen, *Star Names*, p. 329.
[17] Frances Rolleston, *Mazzaroth*, p. 9.

THE BREAKER

Overall, the term breaker in Micah signifies a leader who clears the path, breaks down barriers, and leads the people to a place of deliverance, symbolizing God's intervention and victorious presence in the lives of his people. Doesn't that sound like something we need today, too?

The name of the Breaker is similar to what Jesus said in Luke 4:18 about how he was anointed to "set the captives free" and to "set at liberty those who are oppressed."

> *Luke 4:18 ESV*
> *The Spirit of the Lord is upon me, because he has anointed me to proclaim good news to the poor. He has sent me to proclaim liberty to the captives and recovering of sight to the blind, to set at liberty those who are oppressed.*

This verse is quoted from Isaiah 61:1 and uses the same Hebrew root verb for "break" as in the star name Atik. The verb is *nathaq*. It means to burst the bonds asunder.

> *Isaiah 58:6 ESV*
> *"Is not this the fast that I choose: to loose the bonds of wickedness, to undo the straps of the yoke, to let the oppressed go free, and to break every yoke?*

There are a number of Christian songs today that talk about being freed from chains, but here is a clip of lyrics from Tasha Cobb's song "Break Every Chain."

"There is power in the name of Jesus
There is power in the name of Jesus
(There is power)
There is power in the name of Jesus
(We know where it is)

To break every chain, break every chain, break every chain
To break every chain, break every chain, break every chain."

We know where the power is – in the name of the Deliverer, the Savior and the Breaker. He can rescue anyone from any captivity or prison or oppression.

Acts 10:38 APNT
concerning Jesus, who was from Nazareth, whom God anointed with the Holy Spirit and with power. And this is he who traveled around and healed those who were oppressed by the Evil [one], because God was with him.

> ACTION ITEM: What do you need deliverance from or a breakthrough for? Pray to God in the name of the Breaker for your rescue!

Chapter 12 – The Branch of the Lord

Four inspired accounts of the earthly ministry of the Son of God have been given to us in the four gospels. Each of these gospels provide four distinct aspects of the earthly life and ministry of Christ. The gospel of Matthew sets forth the Lord as KING and traces his genealogy back through David. Mark presents the Savior as a SERVANT. There is no genealogy in the opening chapter, but immediate service, and this feature persists even after the resurrection, the gospel closing with the words, *"The Lord working with them, and confirming the Word with signs following" (Mark 16:20).* Luke sets forth the Lord as the MAN and traces his genealogy back to Adam. The gospel of John begins with pointing out Jesus as the SON OF GOD, and the eight signs throughout the book also point to his authority and power as the judge of man and "the Word made flesh."

There is another fourfold promise that goes back to the days of Adam that must also be fulfilled in Christ as set forth in the four gospels. From the earliest times, the cherubim have been associated with the four gospels. These living ones are described as having four faces and four wings.

> *Ezekiel 1:5-10 ESV*
> *5 And from the midst of it came the likeness of four living creatures. And this was their appearance: they had a human likeness,*
> *6 but each had four faces, and each of them had four wings.*
> *7 Their legs were straight, and the soles of their feet were like the sole of a calf's foot. And they sparkled like burnished bronze.*
> *8 Under their wings on their four sides they had human hands. And the four had their faces and their wings thus:*

91

9 their wings touched one another. Each one of them went straight forward, without turning as they went.
10 As for the likeness of their faces, each had a human face. The four had the face of a lion on the right side, the four had the face of an ox on the left side, and the four had the face of an eagle.

The emblems of the lion, the ox, the man and the eagle are portrayed in the Zodiac as well as were used on the standards of the tribes of Israel for Judah, Ephraim, Reuben and Dan, respectively.

These four titles and representations of the Messiah can be understood by observing the use in the Old Testament of one peculiar title of Jesus, namely "The Branch." The figurative use of a "branch" indicates a notable offspring or descendant. In order to understand this name for the Messiah, it is important to understand how the word "branch" is used in Hebrew. Unlike our English word "branch," which refers strictly to the bough of a tree (and not to the trunk), the Hebrew word for "branch" (*tsemach*) has a broader range of meaning. It means "sprout, shoot, branch, bud, that which grew (upon)." In other words, it can refer to a bough of a tree (whether large or small), or to a whole tree.

There are six times in the Old Testament where the word Branch refers to the Messiah. Five of these uses are with the Hebrew word *tsemach* and one with another word for sprout or shoot, *netser*. The use with *netser* shows that the Messiah will descend from the line of Jesse, the father of David.

Isaiah 11:1 ESV
There shall come forth a shoot from the stump of Jesse, and a branch [netser] from his roots shall bear fruit.

Four of the uses of *tsemach* line up with the four themes of the gospels and the faces of the cherubim. The first reference we will look at is about the KING.

> *Jeremiah 33:15-17 ESV*
> *15 In those days and at that time I will cause a righteous Branch to spring up for David, and he shall execute justice and righteousness in the land.*
> *16 In those days Judah will be saved, and Jerusalem will dwell securely. And this is the name by which it [Jerusalem] will be called: 'The LORD is our righteousness.'*
> *17 "For thus says the LORD: David shall never lack a man to sit on the throne of the house of Israel.*

The Branch, who is the King, is the one who will come from the line of David and bring a righteous rule and justice to Israel. In Matthew, many references are made to the coming "kingdom of heaven" and what it will be like.

The second reference of the Branch is about the servant and corresponds to the gospel of Mark.

> *Zechariah 3:8 ESV*
> *Hear now, O Joshua the high priest, you and your friends who sit before you, for they are men who are a sign: behold, I will bring my servant the Branch.*

There are many references in the Old Testament about the Messiah being a servant. Here is one:

> *Isaiah 42:1 ESV*
> *Behold my servant, whom I uphold, my chosen, in whom my soul delights; I have put my Spirit upon him; he will bring forth justice to the nations.*

The third use of the Branch is about the MAN.

> *Zechariah 6:12-13 ESV*
> *12 And say to him, 'Thus says the LORD of hosts,*
> *"Behold, the man whose name is the Branch: for he shall*
> *branch out from his place, and he shall build the temple*
> *of the LORD.*
> *13 It is he who shall build the temple of the LORD and*
> *shall bear royal honor, and shall sit and rule on his*
> *throne. And there shall be a priest on his throne, and the*
> *counsel of peace shall be between them both."*

The Messiah's job will be to build the temple and function as not only a king but also a high priest. He fulfills this today as the mediator.

> *1 Timothy 2:5-6 ESV*
> *5 For there is one God, and there is one mediator*
> *between God and men, the man Christ Jesus,*
> *6 who gave himself as a ransom for all, which is the*
> *testimony given at the proper time.*

The fourth reference of the Branch is in Isaiah.

> *Isaiah 4:2 ESV*
> *In that day the branch of the LORD shall be beautiful and*
> *glorious, and the fruit of the land shall be the pride and*
> *honor of the survivors of Israel.*

The Messiah will be the Son of God, God's descendant and he will be glorious!

There is another reference of the Branch to the Messiah as king. Why would there be two references to his kingship?

Jeremiah 23:5 ESV
"Behold, the days are coming, declares the LORD, when I will raise up for David a righteous Branch, and he shall reign as king and deal wisely, and shall execute justice and righteousness in the land.

Both this verse and Jeremiah 33:15 speak of the Messiah being a king. My colleague, Giles Fischer, proposes a unique understanding of this. He shows that Matthew is presented as the peaceful shepherd king and that Revelation reveals the Messiah as the warrior king who brings the actual kingdom into fruition. So, the two verses about the king show the coming king and the king coming in reality. Charles Welch, a student of Bullinger, also concurs with this proposal and links Revelation to Matthew.[18]

Coming to the New Testament we find in the opening book, the Gospel of Matthew, a striking and obvious connection between this gospel of the kingdom, and the Revelation. Matthew presents us with the coming of the "Son of man" in lowliness, finally showing us His rejection by Israel as their King, His head crowned with thorns, and the Gentile successor of Nebuchadnezzar's dominion preferred to the King of God's appointment.

The Revelation has an answer to this, just as it had an answer to all that was said in Genesis. In the Revelation the Lord is seen coming again, still as the Son of man, this time in great glory, this time crowned with many crowns, this time to enter into His place as heaven's appointed King to rule with a rod of iron, to overthrow the final blasphemous development of Gentile dominion,

---

[18] Giles Fischer, *The Great Mystery Revealed*, pp. 79-83.

and to usher in that perfect kingdom concerning which all the prophets had spoken.[19]

When Jesus comes as the king in Revelation, he will be the KING of kings and LORD of lords. There will be no other higher or more powerful than he is! A king always has the last word and his word is inviolable – that means it can never be broken, infringed or dishonored. Both verses in Jeremiah describe the coming king, but the second one is stated as though his kingdom is already established and glorious. Oh, what a day that will be!

ACTION ITEM: Declare the word of the King of kings over your life that will absolutely come to pass!

"The Branch" titles for the Messiah have deep meaning. They teach that Jesus is the descendant of David (and King of Israel), that he is the Lord's Servant, that he is a true member of the human family (and of the family of Israel), and that he is the Son of God. "The Branch" title also implies that he will, just like a mighty cedar tree, provide shelter, protection, and nourishment for all the families of mankind, when he sits down on his throne in Mount Zion. Jesus Christ is truly "excellent" and "comely," and all our glorying should be in him.

---

[19] Charles Welch, *This Prophecy*, pp. 1-2.

Chapter 13 – The Light of the World

In the last chapter we discussed the Hebrew word for the Branch. At first glance, the New Testament does not seem to have picked up on the description of Jesus as the Branch. However, Luke 1:78 contains a hidden reference to the branch.

> *Luke 1:76-79 APNT*
> *76 And you, [oh] child, will be called the prophet of the Most High, for you will go before the face of the LORD to prepare his way,*
> *77 so that he may give the knowledge of life to his people in the forgiveness of their sins,*
> *78 by the bowels of mercy of our God, by which the dawn from on high will visit us,*
> *79 to enlighten those who sit in darkness and in the shadows of death, that he may direct our feet in the way of peace."*

This is a prophecy from Zachariah about John the Baptist, his son, and says that John will prepare the way for the "dawn from on high." The word for "dawn" is *anatole* in Greek and *denkha* in Aramaic. Both words mean rising up or dawn or shining. But their secondary meanings are as a shoot or branch. The Septuagint uses *anatole* in four of the references to the Branch in the Old Testament: Jeremiah 23:5, 33:15, Zechariah 3:8 and 6:12. The Peshitta Old Testament uses *denkha* for Zechariah 3:8, 6:12, and Isaiah 4:2. Here is one translation from the Septuagint.

> *Zechariah 6:12 LXX*
> *and thou shalt say to him, Thus saith the Lord Almighty; Behold the man whose name is The Branch [anatole]; and he shall spring up [anatello – the verb] from his stem, and build the house of the Lord.*

The dayspring (as it is translated in the King James Version) from on high who has visited us is the bringer of light, sometimes also called the bright and morning star. Jesus calls himself the "light of the world" in several places, especially in the gospel of John.

> *John 8:12 APNT*
> *Now again Jesus spoke to them and said, "I am the light of the world. He who follows me will not walk in darkness, but he will find for himself the light of life."*

To call Jesus the light is a metaphor, meaning he has the characteristics of light. Light shows the path to walk on, as it said in Luke 1:79: "that he may direct our feet in the way of peace."

Jesus explained to people questioning him that he was bringing light so they would know where they were going.

> *John 12:35-41 NET*
> *35 Jesus replied, "The light is with you for a little while longer. Walk while you have the light, so that the darkness may not overtake you. The one who walks in the darkness does not know where he is going.*
> *36 While you have the light, believe in the light, so that you may become sons of light." When Jesus had said these things, he went away and hid himself from them.*
> *37 Although Jesus had performed so many miraculous signs before them, they still refused to believe in him,*
> *38 so that the word of Isaiah the prophet would be fulfilled. He said, "Lord, who has believed our message, and to whom has the arm of the Lord been revealed?"*
> *39 For this reason they could not believe, because again Isaiah said,*

40 "He has blinded their eyes and hardened their heart, so that they would not see with their eyes and understand with their heart, and turn to me, and I would heal them."
41 Isaiah said these things because he saw Christ's glory, and spoke about him.

Light chases the darkness away. Not only does it expose, but it also refreshes, warms and causes good fruit. Ephesians explains what light does and how to walk in it.

Ephesians 5:8-14 ESV
8 for at one time you were darkness, but now you are light in the Lord. Walk as children of light
9 (for the fruit of light is found in all that is good and right and true),
10 and try to discern what is pleasing to the Lord.
11 Take no part in the unfruitful works of darkness, but instead expose them.
12 For it is shameful even to speak of the things that they do in secret.
13 But when anything is exposed by the light, it becomes visible,
14 for anything that becomes visible is light. Therefore it says, "Awake, O sleeper, and arise from the dead, and Christ will shine on you."

Jesus also said that he is the Light of the WORLD. He shines into the darkness of the whole world and all the people in it to not only expose the darkness, but to bring people into the light. What an apropos title for the Lord! Everyone can have this freedom to walk in the light as children of light.

ACTION ITEM: Let your light shine on someone new today and talk about the glory of God in the face of Jesus Christ.

Chapter 14 – The Last Adam

Jesus Christ is made in the image of God, as Adam was. In this chapter we will see that this description and title for Jesus is based on the first creation of mankind in Genesis.

> *Genesis 1:26-27 NET*
> *26 Then God said, "Let us make humankind in our image, after our likeness, so they may rule over the fish of the sea and the birds of the air, over the cattle, and over all the earth, and over all the creatures that move on the earth."*
> *27 God created humankind in his own image, in the image of God he created them, male and female he created them.*

There are three words that are important in this passage: image, likeness and rule. The word for image in Hebrew is *tselem*. It can mean an image, a likeness, a statue, a model or a shadow. A shadow would show the outline and details of the original, but not all the actual reality of it. Man was created in the image of God with his primary image being Spirit. "God's image obviously does not consist in man's body which was formed from earthly matter, but in his spiritual, intellectual, moral likeness to God…"[20]

The second word, likeness, is *demuth* in Hebrew. It has more to do with abstract concepts like characteristics and traits. We can see that in the meaning for "like." If a man has a son, often his looks and character are similar. Both words are used when Adam had a son named Seth.

---

[20] *Theological Wordbook of the Old Testament*, image 1923a.

Genesis 5:3 ESV
When Adam had lived 130 years, he fathered a son in his
own likeness [demuth], after his image [tselem], and
named him Seth.

There are three words built with the letters *daleth-mem*: *dam*
meaning blood, *adam* meaning red and *demuth* meaning
likeness. The blood of Adam contained his soul and also this
"likeness" to God (Leviticus 17:11). The faculties for logic,
reasoning, communication and other characteristics of God
are what gave man the ability to "rule" over all the other
animals and creation.

Genesis 1:28 NET
God blessed them and said to them, "Be fruitful and
multiply! Fill the earth and subdue it! Rule over the fish
of the sea and the birds of the air and every creature that
moves on the ground."

The New English Translation notes describe the word for
"subdue" as follows: "The general meaning of the verb
appears to be 'to bring under one's control for one's
advantage.' In Gen 1:28 one might paraphrase it as follows:
'harness its potential and use its resources for your benefit.'"

Furthermore, God said that man would rule or have dominion
over all creatures. He was given the image and likeness of God
in order to be able to do this. Man is capable of being God's
representative and shares in the authority of God's creation.
That was God's design. He made man a little lower than God
so that this could happen. The word for "heavenly beings" is
Elohim meaning God.

Psalm 8:3-8 ESV
3 When I look at your heavens, the work of your fingers,
the moon and the stars, which you have set in place,
4 what is man that you are mindful of him, and the son of
man that you care for him?
5 Yet you have made him a little lower than the heavenly
beings and crowned him with glory and honor.
6 You have given him dominion over the works of your
hands; you have put all things under his feet,
7 all sheep and oxen, and also the beasts of the field,
8 the birds of the heavens, and the fish of the sea,
whatever passes along the paths of the seas.

Of course, then in the fall of Adam and Eve, this image and likeness was corrupted because of the introduction of sin. However, because of the principle of "everything after its kind," God was able to send a man who was in the image of God also, but who was without sin in order to redeem mankind and restore their rightful place of dominion over the earth.

Haven't you ever thought that it was such a terrible thing that every person who has ever lived from the progeny of Adam had to bear the sin nature that he had? I have! But actually, God in his foreknowledge knew that once there was another man made in the image of God, he would be able to transfer the nature of that man to everyone who believed on him. Let's look at this from the New Testament.

Hebrews 1:2-5 APNT
2 And in these last days, he has spoken to us by his Son,
whom he appointed heir of everything and by whom he
made the ages,
3 who is the radiance of his glory and the image of his
being and almighty by the power of his word. And in his

person, he accomplished the cleansing of our sins and sat down at the right hand of majesty in the high places.
4 And this [one] is greater than the angels in every way, even as the name that he inherited is greater than theirs.
5 For to which of the angels did God ever say: YOU ARE MY SON, THIS DAY I HAVE FATHERED YOU, and again, I WILL BE A FATHER TO HIM AND HE WILL BE A SON TO ME?

The word for image in Hebrews 1 is not the same as in Genesis. It means "character." The image that God gave to Jesus was a son in complete likeness to his Father God. Jesus is the firstborn of many brothers.

Colossians 1:12-18 APNT
12 you should give thanks to God the Father, who has made us worthy for a portion of the inheritance of the holy [ones] in light
13 and has delivered us from the authority of darkness and has transferred us to the kingdom of his beloved Son,
14 in whom we have redemption and forgiveness of sins,
15 who is the image of the God who is not seen and the firstborn of all created [ones].
16 And in him everything that is in heaven and on earth was built, all that is seen and all that is not seen, whether thrones or lordships or rulers or authorities, everything [is] by way of him and was built in him.
17 And he is in front of all and everything stands in him.
18 And he is the head of the body, the church, for he is the beginning and the firstborn from the dead in order that he would be the first in all [things].

Jesus Christ is the first in all things and as the "beloved Son" he has been given dominion again over all in heaven and earth which is even more than what Adam had. And he has made it possible for all who believe on him to have life through him.

1 Corinthians 15:20-26 APNT
20 But now Christ has risen from the dead and has become the first of those asleep.
21 And as by way of a man came death, so also by way of a man came the resurrection of the dead.
22 For as in Adam all men die, so also in Christ all live,
23 each in his order. Christ was the first [and] after that, those who are of Christ at his coming.
24 And then will be the end, when he delivers the kingdom to God the Father, when every ruler and every authority and all powers cease.
25 For he is going to reign, until he places all his enemies under his feet.
26 And the last enemy, death, will be abolished.

Not only are these wonderful truths available about Jesus Christ, but because we are in Christ, we are conformed to the image of his Son and become image bearers of God, too.

Romans 8:29 APNT
And from the first he knew them and marked them out with the likeness of the image of his Son, that he would be the firstborn of many brothers.

This leads us to how we can use this title of the "image of God" in our lives.

2 Corinthians 3:17-18 APNT
17 Now the LORD is the Spirit and where the Spirit of the LORD [is], there is freedom.
18 But all of us, with open faces, see the magnificence of the LORD as in a mirror and we are being changed into

that likeness from glory to glory, as by the LORD, the Spirit.

We can become "glory reflectors" of who God is. The mirror is a reflection of who we truly are. God is love, light, holy, kind, faithful, full of compassion, long-suffering, forgiving, full of peace, to only name a few things of his character. All those characteristics are part of his image in his Son in us. Now we can shine out the glorious gospel of how God made Jesus in his image and has now made available the same thing for us!

2 Corinthians 4:3-7 NET
3 But even if our gospel is veiled, it is veiled only to those who are perishing,
4 among whom the god of this age has blinded the minds of those who do not believe so they would not see the light of the glorious gospel of Christ, who is the image of God.
5 For we do not proclaim ourselves, but Jesus Christ as Lord, and ourselves as your slaves for Jesus' sake.
6 For God, who said "Let light shine out of darkness," is the one who shined in our hearts to give us the light of the glorious knowledge of God in the face of Christ.
7 But we have this treasure in clay jars, so that the extraordinary power belongs to God and does not come from us.

ACTION ITEM: Praise God for his matchless wisdom in designing man the way he did, even knowing that Adam would sin. Ask God to help us understand how to reflect his glory.

Chapter 15 – Conclusion

As you have probably noticed, there are not many personal testimonies of using the name of Jesus in this book. The reason is that it was my prayer that the chapters would remind you of incidents in your own life when there was change because of using the name of Jesus. He does change things!

I want to conclude the book with reviewing what it means to stand in the gap for someone. We touched on it in the chapter on "His name is Wonderful" how Jesus as the high priest is our intercessor. But now we can be intercessors too and by using the authority of his name, we can make up a hole in the hedge.

STANDING IN THE GAP

> *Ezekiel 22:30 KJV*
> *And I sought for a man among them, that should make up the hedge, and stand in the gap before me for the land, that I should not destroy it: but I found none.*

Standing in the gap is just a different picture of how you can surround people with love. And in the process of that surrounding, people get healed of fear and any other need they have and the hole in the hedge is filled in. When someone has a need, we can put them in the middle of the family so to speak and surround them with love. We surround them with prayer, with the name of Jesus Christ, with ministering, with teaching or whatever they need.

I thought for many years that it had to be about my faith. And then I would ask God why I didn't see signs, miracles and wonders like in the first century. Then I went to Romania and I saw gypsies minister to each other and they didn't know anything about the Bible at all! All they knew was that God loved them and they started ministering that love to each other and people would just get healed immediately. We saw this over and over and when I came back to the United States, I wanted to see how to teach this from scripture. That's what led me to Ezekiel 22.

God is talking in verse 30 about how there was a hole in the hedge and he was looking for someone who would come to fill it in and he couldn't find anybody. To make up the hedge means to restore the wall, as though there's actually a hole in the wall. When someone has fear or they're sick or they're emotionally worked up about whatever, there's a hole in the fence. And what we need to do is go to stand in the gap.

God says, "I looked for a man to stand in the gap before me." When we minister to someone, this is what we're doing. We're going to go stand in the gap because there's a hole, but we have to go stand before God, not before the problem. We actually have to turn away from the problem and look totally away from the problem and only look to God and the Lord Jesus Christ.

I want to give you an example of how Jesus did this and thus how we can too from Mark chapter 9. It is about the father who had an epileptic child and brought him to the disciples to be healed and the disciples couldn't heal him. In the meantime, Jesus had been up on the Mount of Transfiguration. When he saw the crowd, Jesus asked what was going on and the father came to talk with Jesus.

Mark 9:17-18 APNT
17 And one of the crowd answered and said, "Teacher, I brought my son to you, because he has a spirit that does not speak.

---

18 And sometimes it grabs him, it knocks him down and he foams and gnashes his teeth and he languishes. And I asked your disciples to cast it out, and they were not able."

So now you first see that part of the reason why the disciples could not heal him is that the disciples were looking at the problem. The boy is wallowing on the ground. All these people are staring at them. The scribes and Pharisees are accusing them: "Why can't you heal him? What's the matter with you?" It is not surprising because when someone is questioning your authority, it is easy to question yourself. But here is how Jesus answered.

Mark 9:19-20 APNT
19 Jesus answered and said to him, "Oh faithless generation! How long must I be with you and how long must I endure you? Bring him to me."
20 And they brought him to him. And when the spirit saw him, immediately it knocked him down and he fell on the ground and was violently shaken, and he foamed.

The spirit tries the same thing when Jesus comes on the scene. Jesus does not pay any attention to the wallowing, but turns to the father.

Mark 9:21-22 APNT
21 And Jesus asked his father, "How long [has it been] since [he was] this way?" He said to him, "Since his youth.
22 And many times it has thrown him into the fire and into the water to destroy him, but whatever you are able [to do], help me and have compassion on us."

And Jesus calmly turns to ask the father. "Oh, by the way, how long has it been since this started?" You can see here that the father was looking at the problem. That's all he could see. And we can have great compassion for that man because if it was your child and you were in this situation, it would be extremely difficult not to be looking at the problem, especially because it had gone on for a long time.

Jesus immediately took the father's attention off of the problem. Here's his child doing all this in front of everybody, right? And Jesus helps the father to focus on him. That's why we need each other. When somebody is close to you and you haven't been able to deal with the problem yourself, that is the time to go to involve the greater body of Christ. Our brothers and sisters are not so intimately close to the problem and they can do what Jesus did here. You can do what Jesus did.

Verse 23 is the key to understanding this passage.

> *Mark 9:23 APNT*
> *Jesus said to him, "If you are able to believe, everything will be possible to him who believes."*

I have heard a lot of teachings on this verse that Jesus is requiring the father to have faith. If he could believe everything would be possible. But that's not what the verse actually says. The word believe is not in the majority of the early manuscripts. And it's almost an exclamation point that Jesus says, "If you can!" The New English Translation has this correctly rendered.

> *Mark 9:23 NET*
> *Then Jesus said to him, " 'If you are able?' All things are possible for the one who believes."*

Jesus turns the father's words back towards him saying, "If you can look at me, I can believe for this to happen. If you just look at me, then everything is possible." Nothing is impossible if we look to Jesus to be the one who has the faith. And so that's when immediately the father of the boy cries out and it says he was mourning because nobody had ever told him that before.

Mark 9:24 APNT
And immediately the father of the boy cried out, mourning, and said, "I believe, my Lord! Help the lack of my faith."

Help means to rescue, come to the aid of. The father was saying in essence, I believe you can heal my boy!

Mark 9:25-27 APNT
25 And when Jesus saw that the people ran and gathered about him, he rebuked that unclean spirit and said to it, "Dumb spirit that does not speak, I command you, come out of him and do not enter him again."
26 And that demon cried out and he bruised him much and came out. And he was like a dead man, so that many said, "He is dead."
27 But Jesus took him by his hand and raised him up.

Jesus demanded faith in his authority to heal and then because the man was able to respond to that, grace was poured out and the boy got healed. Jesus also nipped it in the bud when more people came running to give their opinion. Jesus continued to stay his mind on God and on his answers. That's how he made up the hole in the hedge.

Mark 9:28-29 APNT
28 Now when Jesus entered the house, his disciples asked him privately, "Why were we not able to cast it out?"
29 He said to them, "This kind cannot be cast out by anything except by fasting and by prayer."

111

CONCLUSION

Jesus is not talking about fasting and not eating. What is the true fasting? True fasting is to make up whatever the difference is so that the person can believe. It includes building up the wall, letting the oppressed go free, doing everything and anything that it takes to help a person believe, teaching them the truth and showing them the error of whatever it is that they are not believing. It could also include proclaiming testimonies about other people so that they can believe.

Isaiah 58:6-12 ESV
6 "Is not this the fast that I choose: to loose the bonds of wickedness, to undo the straps of the yoke, to let the oppressed go free, and to break every yoke?
7 Is it not to share your bread with the hungry and bring the homeless poor into your house; when you see the naked, to cover him, and not to hide yourself from your own flesh?
8 Then shall your light break forth like the dawn, and your healing shall spring up speedily; your righteousness shall go before you; the glory of the LORD shall be your rear guard.
9 Then you shall call, and the LORD will answer; you shall cry, and he will say, 'Here I am.' If you take away the yoke from your midst, the pointing of the finger, and speaking wickedness,
10 if you pour yourself out for the hungry and satisfy the desire of the afflicted, then shall your light rise in the darkness and your gloom be as the noonday.
11 And the LORD will guide you continually and satisfy your desire in scorched places and make your bones strong; and you shall be like a watered garden, like a spring of water, whose waters do not fail.
12 And your ancient ruins shall be rebuilt; you shall raise up the foundations of many generations; you shall be

CONCLUSION

called the repairer of the breach, the restorer of streets to dwell in."

Go in with authority using the name of Jesus Christ. Stand in the gap and build up the wall. You fill in that which is missing. Put up the shield of faith because it quenches ALL the fiery darts of the wicked one. Let's lock our shields together and use the name that changes everything!

THE MASTER KEY

Now that we have seen so many names and titles that belong to Jesus, the Anointed One, our Lord, I want to go back to the beginning chapter about the authority we have to use the name of Jesus. I had mentioned that it was like having a power of attorney to do business on someone's behalf. It is also like having a master key for a whole property or the use of a code to get in someone's garage. Once you have a master key or the code, you have access to everything in that property.

Have you ever looked at your keychain and wondered what on earth that key goes to? It has stayed with your other keys for such a long time that you actually have forgotten what it is for! But that's because you don't use it very often or at all. But when you use a key regularly, it becomes very important to keep it on your person at all times. That is the same thing with the name of Jesus. It is our master key to getting answers to prayer and we need to use it in many different situations.

In many of the Action Items in the chapters, we have seen that it is important to apply specific ways we can use Jesus' name. Because he has delegated the power to us to use his name, he says that we need to ask and it will be given to us.

John 15:7-16 APNT
7 But if you remain in me and my words remain in you,
whatever you want to ask, you will have.
8 In this the Father is glorified, that you bear much fruit
and be my disciples.
9 As my Father has loved me, so also I have loved you.
Remain in my compassion.
10 If you keep my commandments, you will remain in my
love, as I have kept the commandments of my Father and
remain in his love.
11 These [things] I have spoken with you, so that my joy
would be in you and [that] your joy would be made full.
12 This is my commandment, that you love one another
as I have loved you.
13 There is no love that is greater than this, that a man
would lay down his life for his friends.
14 You are my friends, if you do all that I command you.
15 No longer do I call you servants, because a servant
does not know what his lord does, but I have called you
my friends, because everything that I have heard from my
Father I have made known to you.
16 You did not choose me, but I have chosen you and I
have appointed you that you also should go [and] bear
fruit and [that] your fruit should remain, so that whatever
you ask of my Father in my name, he will give to you.

In the evening before Jesus' trial, he explained to the disciples
that he was going to send a Comforter to them and that after
he was gone, they would still have access to him by way of
the Spirit.

John 16:23-24 APNT
23 And in that day you will not ask me anything. Truly,
truly I say to you, everything that you ask of my Father in
my name, he will give to you.

CONCLUSION

24 Until now you have not asked for anything in my name.
Ask and you will receive, so that your joy may be full.

The reason we need to ask in Jesus' name is not only that it changes every situation, but it is so your joy may be full. Some other translations say, "that your joy may be complete." I know that in various situations, when using the name of Jesus, and the prayers got answered, there was so much joy! We realize that the "excellency of the power is of God and not of us" (2 Corinthians 4:7).

Reverend Kenneth Hagin sums up our power base in the name of Jesus like this:

> Jesus' Name has the power to get things done – in Heaven, in earth, and under the earth. Because of the position He holds—and because His Name was received by inheritance, bestowal and conquest – His is the Name that's above every name! At the Name of Jesus, everything that has a name must bow. All of your problems have names; therefore, they must bow to the Name of Jesus. (If you're not shouting about that fact, it's not real to you yet!)

> Say this out loud: "Jesus received His Name by inheritance, by bestowal, and by conquest. I have a right to use that Name. By the shed blood of the Lord Jesus Christ, I have power of attorney to use that Name. I'm going to walk forth and shout the Name of Jesus every time the devil raises his head. The devil is under my feet because of the Name of Jesus."[21]

---

[21] Kenneth Hagin, *Jesus, Name Above All Names*, p. 49.

115

CONCLUSION

Jesus' name means deliverer! He is the deliverance for every situation that needs changing. Let's continue to use HIS NAME in our own lives, as well as for others! Jesus Christ our Lord is the name that changes everything!

Alphabet Chart

Hebrew Name	Hebrew Script	Aramaic Name	Aramaic Script	Ancient Pictograph
Aleph	א	Alaph	✦	४
Beyt	ב	Beth	ג	⊡
Gimel	ג	Gamel	ג	⌐
Dalet	ד	Daleth	৯	⊤
Hey	ה	He	ক	유
Vav	ו	Wau	ঌ	Y
Zayin	ז	Zain	'	⊏
Chet	ח	Kheth	ৣ	⊞
Tet	ט	Teth	↴	⊗
Yud	י	Yoth	↵	⊣
Kaph	כ	Kaph	↳	⨆
Lamed	ל	Lamed	↳	∪
Mem	מ	Mem	ಶ	⋀
Nun	נ	Nun	↵	⎘
Samech	ס	Semkath	♨	≸
Ayin	ע	Ai	↳	⊙
Pey	פ	Pey	ঌ	⊖
Tsade	צ	Tzaddi	ৼ	⌒
Quph	ק	Qoph	◻	⊕
Resh	ר	Resh	ⵎ	ঀ
Shin	ש	Shin	⊐	⊔
Tav	ת	Tau	ঌ	†

Master Chart of Pictographs

Ancient Pictograph	Simple Meaning	Alternate Meaning	Verbs	Nouns	Prep/Adj	Notes
ox symbol	ox		be strong, lead	strong one, leader	chief	
house symbol	house, tent			family, house	in, inside, with, by	
neck symbol	neck of camel	foot	gather, walk, lift up, carry, reward	recompense		
door symbol	door		enter, move, divide	door, gate, curtain, entrance	of	
man with arms raised symbol	man with arms raised	window	behold, reveal, look	breath		at end of word, used as definite article or "what comes from"
tent peg symbol	tent peg		add, connect, join	nail, hook	and, but	in middle of word, changes incomplete to completed action
ax symbol	ax, plough	weapon	cut, harvest	weapon, enemy, food		
fence symbol	fence, tent wall		divide, separate	fence, wall	inside or outside	
basket symbol	basket	snake	surround, contain		surrounding	
arm and hand symbol	arm and hand		work, throw, do	power		suffix: me, my
open palm symbol	open palm of hand		bend, open, allow, cover	palm, hollow, source		suffix: you, your
staff symbol	staff (shepherd)	ox goad	guide, teach, lead	shepherding, authority, comfort	to, for	
water symbol	water		flow	spiritual life, sustenance		first letter: turns verb into noun
seed symbol	seed	fish	sprout, grow	life, continuity		suffix: we, our
thorn symbol	thorn, prop		support, protect	protection		
eye symbol	eye		see, watch, know, experience			
open mouth symbol	open mouth		say, speak, open	opening		
man lying symbol	man lying on his side	fishing hook	hunt, search, need, seek			first letter: all the way to a specific end
sun on horizon symbol	sun on horizon	back of head	rise up, follow, go around	circle, arch	after	
man head symbol	man, head			man, person beginning	first	
teeth symbol	teeth, breasts		press, fill, change, consume	source of life, fullness		first letter: turns a verb into person who does action
crossed sticks symbol	crossed sticks		end	mark, sign, ownership		first letter means "observed"

118

Names and Titles of Jesus

Adam	1 Corinthians 15:45
Advocate	1 John 2:1
Amen	Revelation 3:14
Anointed	Psalm 2:2
Apostle	Hebrews 3:1
Arm of the Lord	Isaiah 51:9-10
Author and finisher of our faith	Hebrews 12:2
Beloved	Ephesians 1:6
Branch	Jeremiah 23:5; Zechariah 3:8
Bread of life	John 6:48
Bridegroom	Matthew 9:15
Bright and morning star	Revelation 22:16
Brightness of the Father's glory	Hebrews 1:3
Captain of the Lord's host	Joshua 5:14, 15
Captain of salvation	Hebrews 2:10
Chief Shepherd	1 Peter 5:4
Chief corner stone	1 Peter 2:6
Chosen of God	1 Peter 2:4
The Christ	Matthew 16:20; Mark 14:61
Christ, a King	Luke 23:2

NAMES AND TITLES OF JESUS

Christ Jesus	Acts 19:4; Romans 3:24
Christ Jesus our Lord	Romans 8:39; 1 Timothy 1:12
Christ of God	Luke 9:20
Christ, the chosen of God	Luke 23:35
Christ the Lord	Luke 2:11
Christ the power of God	1 Corinthians 1:24
Christ the wisdom of God	1 Corinthians 1:24
Christ, the Son of God	Acts 9:20
Christ, Son of the Blessed	Mark 14:61
Commander	Isaiah 55:4
Consolation of Israel	Luke 2:25
Cornerstone	Ephesians 2:20
Counsellor	Isaiah 9:6
Covenant of the people	Isaiah 42:6
David	Jeremiah 30:9
Daysman	Job 9:33
Dayspring	Luke 1:78
Day star	2 Peter 1:19
Deliverer	Romans 11:26
Desire of all nations	Haggai 2:7
Door	John 10:7
Elect	Isaiah 42:1

NAMES AND TITLES OF JESUS

Emmanuel	Isaiah 7:14
Ensign	Isaiah 11:10
Faithful and True	Revelation 19:11
Faithful and true witness	Revelation 3:14
Finisher of faith	Hebrews 12:2
First and last	Revelation 1:17; Revelation 2:8; Revelation 22:13
First begotten	Hebrews 1:6
First begotten of the dead	Revelation 1:5
Firstborn	Psalm 89:27
Foundation	Isaiah 28:16
Fountain	Zechariah 13:1
Forerunner	Hebrews 6:20
Friend of publicans and sinners	Matthew 11:19
Gift of God	John 4:10
Glory of Israel	Luke 2:32
Good Master	Matthew 19:16
Governor	Matthew 2:6
Great shepherd of the sheep	Hebrews 13:20
Head of the church	Ephesians 5:23
Heir of all things	Hebrews 1:2
High priest	Hebrews 4:14
Head of every man	1 Corinthians 11:3

NAMES AND TITLES OF JESUS

Head of the body, the church	Colossians 1:18
Head of the corner	Matthew 21:42
Holy child Jesus	Acts 4:30
Holy One	Psalm 16:10; Acts 3:14
Holy one of God	Mark 1:24
Holy one of Israel	Isaiah 41:14; Isaiah 54:5
Holy thing	Luke 1:35
Hope (our)	1 Timothy 1:1
Horn of salvation	Luke 1:69
I Am	John 8:58
Image of his person	Hebrews 1:3
Israel	Isaiah 49:3
Jesus	Matthew 1:21
Jesus Christ	Matthew 1:1; John 1:17
Jesus Christ our Lord	Romans 1:3; 6:11, 23; 1 Corinthians 1:2
Jesus Christ our Savior	Titus 3:6
Jesus of Nazareth	Mark 1:24; Luke 24:19
Jesus of Nazareth, King of the Jews	John 19:19
Jesus, the King of the Jews	Matthew 27:37
Jesus, the Son of God	Hebrews 4:14
Jesus, the son of Joseph	John 6:42
Judge of quick and dead	Acts 10:42

NAMES AND TITLES OF JESUS

Just man	Matthew 27:19
Just One	Acts 7:52; Acts 22:14
Just person	Matthew 27:24
King	Matthew 21:5
King of Israel	John 1:49
King of the Jews	Matthew 2:2
King of saints [or ages]	Revelation 15:3
King of kings	1 Timothy 6:15; Revelation 17:14
King of glory	Psalm 24:7-10
King [of Zion]	Matthew 21:5
King over all the earth	Zechariah 14:9
Lamb	Revelation 5:6, 8
Lamb of God	John 1:29
Lawgiver	Isaiah 33:22
Leader	Isaiah 55:4
Light of the world	John 8:12
Light, everlasting	Isaiah 60:20
Light of the Gentiles	Isaiah 42:6
Light, true	John 1:9
Living bread	John 6:51
Living stone	1 Peter 2:4
Lion of the tribe of Judah	Revelation 5:5

NAMES AND TITLES OF JESUS

Lord	Romans 1:3
Lord of lords	Revelation 17:14; Revelation 19:16
Lord of all	Acts 10:36
Lord and Savior Jesus Christ	2 Peter 1:11; 3:18
Lord Christ	Colossians 3:24
Lord Jesus	Acts 7:59; Colossians 3:17; 1 Thessalonians 4:2
Lord Jesus Christ	Acts 16:31; James 2:1
Lord Jesus Christ our Savior	Titus 1:4
Lord of glory	James 2:1
Lord, both of the dead and living	Romans 14:9
Lord of the Sabbath	Mark 2:28
Lord over all	Romans 10:12
Lord's Christ	Luke 2:26
Man Christ Jesus	1 Timothy 2:5
Man of sorrows	Isaiah 53:3
Master	Matthew 23:8
Mediator	1 Timothy 2:5
Messenger of the covenant	Malachi 3:1
Messiah	John 1:41
Messiah the Prince	Daniel 9:25
Mighty one of Israel	Isaiah 30:29

NAMES AND TITLES OF JESUS

Mighty one of Jacob	Isaiah 49:26
Mighty to save	Isaiah 63:1
Minister of the sanctuary	Hebrews 8:2
Morning star	Revelation 22:16
Most holy	Daniel 9:24
Most mighty	Psalm 45:3
Nazarene	Matthew 2:23
Offspring of David	Revelation 22:16
Only begotten	John 1:14
Only begotten of the Father	John 1:14
Only begotten Son	John 1:18
Passover	1 Corinthians 5:7
Plant of renown	Ezekiel 34:29
Potentate	1 Timothy 6:15
Power of God	1 Corinthians 1:24
Physician	Matthew 9:12
Precious corner stone	Isaiah 28:16
Priest	Hebrews 7:17
Prince	Acts 5:31
Prince of life	Acts 3:15
Prince of peace	Isaiah 9:6
Prince of the kings of the earth	Revelation 1:5

NAMES AND TITLES OF JESUS

Prophet	Deuteronomy 18:15; Matthew 21:11; Luke 24:19
Propitiation	1 John 2:2
Rabbi	John 1:49
Rabboni	John 20:16
Ransom	1 Timothy 2:6
Redeemer	Isaiah 59:20
Resurrection and life	John 11:25
Redemption	1 Corinthians 1:30
Righteous branch	Jeremiah 23:5
Righteous judge	2 Timothy 4:8
Righteous servant	Isaiah 53:11
Righteousness	1 Corinthians 1:30
Rock	1 Corinthians 10:4
Rock of offence	1 Peter 2:8
Root of David	Revelation 5:5; Revelation 22:16
Root of Jesse	Isaiah 11:10
Rose of Sharon	Song of Solomon 2:1
Ruler in Israel	Micah 5:2
Salvation	Luke 2:30
Sanctification	1 Corinthians 1:30
Sanctuary	Isaiah 8:14

NAMES AND TITLES OF JESUS

Savior	Luke 2:11
Savior Jesus Christ	2 Timothy 1:10; Titus 2:13; 2 Peter 1:1
Savior of the body	Ephesians 5:23
Savior of the world	1 John 4:14
Second man	1 Corinthians 15:47
Seed of David	2 Timothy 2:8
Seed of the woman	Genesis 3:15
Servant	Isaiah 42:1
Servant of rulers	Isaiah 49:7
Shepherd	Mark 14:27
Shepherd and bishop of your souls	1 Peter 2:25
Shepherd, chief	1 Peter 5:4
Shepherd, good	John 10:11
Shepherd, great	Hebrews 13:20
Shepherd of Israel	Psalm 80:1
Shiloh	Genesis 49:10
Son of the Father	2 John 1:3
Son of the blessed	Mark 14:61
Son of the highest	Luke 1:32
Son of David	Matthew 9:27
Star and Scepter	Numbers 24:17
Sun of righteousness	Malachi 4:2

NAMES AND TITLES OF JESUS

Stone of stumbling	1 Peter 2:8
Sure foundation	Isaiah 28:16
Teacher	John 3:2
True vine	John 15:1
Unspeakable gift	2 Corinthians 9:15
Very Christ	Acts 9:22
Way, Truth and the Life	John 14:6
Which is, which was, which is to come	Revelation 1:4
Wisdom of God	1 Corinthians 1:24
Witness	Isaiah 55:4; Revelation 1:5
Wonderful	Isaiah 9:6
Word	John 1:1
Word of God	Revelation 19:13
Word of life	1 John 1:1

Bibliography

Allen, Richard Hinckley. *Star Names, Their Lore and Meaning.* New York: Dover Publications, 1963.

Bailey, Kenneth E. *The Good Shepherd.* Downers Grove, Illinois: IVP Academic, 2014.

Barnes, Albert. *Barnes' Notes on the Bible.* Kregel Classics, 1962.

Benner, Jeff A. *The Ancient Hebrew Language and Alphabet.* College Station, Texas: Virtualbookworm.com Publishing, 2005.

Benner, Jeff A. *The Ancient Hebrew Lexicon of the Bible.* College Station, Texas: Virtualbookworm.com Publishing, 2005.

Bridge, Donald. *Why Four Gospels?* Ross-shire, Scotland: Christian Focus Publications, 1996.

Brown, Francis, S.R. Driver, Charles A. Briggs, eds. *The New Brown-Driver-Briggs-Gesenius Hebrew and English Lexicon.* Christian Copyrights, Inc., 1983.

Bullinger, E. W. *A Critical Lexicon and Concordance to the English and Greek New Testament.* Grand Rapids, Michigan: Zondervan Publishing House, 1975.

Bullinger, E. W. *Figures of Speech Used in the Bible.* Grand Rapids, Michigan: Baker Book House, 1968.

Bullinger, E. W. *The Witness of the Stars.* Grand Rapids, Michigan: Kregel Publications, 1967.

Clarke, Adam. *The New Testament of our Lord and Saviour Jesus Christ, Commentary on the Bible.* New York: Abingdon Press. Volumes 1-6.

Evans, Tony. The Power of Jesus' Names. Eugene, Oregon: Harvest House Publishers, 2019.

Fischer, Giles. *The Great Mystery Revealed.* Clarksburg, West Virginia: Para Enterprises Press, 2023.

BIBLIOGRAPHY

Girdlestone, Robert Baker. *Synonyms of the Old Testament.* Grand Rapids, Michigan: Wm. B. Eerdmans Publishing Company, 1897.

Hagin, Kenneth W. *Jesus Name Above all Names.* Tulsa, Oklahoma: Rhema Bible Church, 1998.

Harris, R. Laird, Gleason L. Archer, Jr., Bruce K. Waltke, eds. *Theological Wordbook of the Old Testament* 2 volumes. Chicago, Illinois: Moody Press, 1980.

Horton, T.C., Hurlburt, Charles E. *Names of Christ.* Chicago: Moody Press, 1994.

Jennings, William. *Lexicon to the Syriac New Testament.* London: Oxford University Press, 1926.

Keach, Benjamin. *Tropologia: Key to Open Scripture Metaphors.* London: William Hill Collingridge, City Press, 1856.

Keil, Carl Frederick, Delitzsch, Franz. *Commentary on the Old Testament.* 1976.

Keller, W. Philip. *A Shepherd Looks at Psalm 23.* Grand Rapids, Michigan: Zondervan Publishing House, 2007.

Kenyon, E.W. *The Wonderful Name of Jesus.* Lynnwood, Washington: Kenyon Gospel Publishing Society, 1964.

Klein, Ernest. *A Comprehensive Etymological Dictionary of the Hebrew Language for Readers of English.* University of Haifa, Israel, 1987.

Lightfoot, John. *A Commentary on the New Testament from the Talmud and Hebraica. 4 vols.* Peabody, Massachusetts: Hendrickson Publishers, 1989.

Magiera, Janet M. *The Fence of Salvation.* Colorado Springs, Colorado: LWM Publications, 2018.

McClintock and Strong. *Cyclopedia of Biblical, Theological, and Ecclesiastical Literature.* Grand Rapids, Michigan: Baker Academic, 1982.

BIBLIOGRAPHY

Murdock, James, trans. *The New Testament*. New York: Stanford and Swords, 1852.

Richards, Lawrence O. *New International Encyclopedia of Bible Words*. Grand Rapids, Michigan: Zondervan Publishing House, 1991.

Richardson, Alan, ed. *A Theological Word Book of the Bible*. New York: Macmillan Publishing Co, 1950.

Rolleston, Frances. *Mazzaroth*. York Beach, Maine: Weiser Books, 2001.

Ryken, Leland, ed. *Dictionary of Biblical Imagery*. Downers Grove, Illinois: InterVarsity Press, 1998.

Seekins, Frank T. *Hebrew Word Pictures*. Frank T. Seekins, 2012.

Smith, J. Payne. *A Compendious Syriac Dictionary*. London: Oxford at the Clarendon Press, 1967.

Sokoloff, Michael. *A Syriac Lexicon*. Winona Lake, Indiana: Eisenbrauns, 2009.

Thayer, Joseph Henry. *The New Thayer's Greek-English Lexicon*. Christian Copyrights, Inc., 1983.

Webster, Noah. *Noah Webster's First Edition of an American Dictionary of the English Language*. San Francisco: Foundation for American Christian Education, 1967.

Welch, Charles H. *This Prophecy*. Berean Publishing Trust, 1984.

Williams, David J. Paul's Metaphors Their Context and Character. Peabody, Massachusetts: Hendrickson Publishers, Inc., 1999.

Wolff, Hans Walter. *Anthropology of the Old Testament*. Philadelphia: Fortress Press, 1974.

About the Author

Janet Magiera is an ordained minister and the founder of Light of the Word Ministry, a ministry dedicated to teaching and making known the understanding of the Aramaic language, figures of speech and customs of the Bible. In 1979, under the tutelage of a student of Dr. George M. Lamsa, Jan began pursuing a course of study of the Aramaic Peshitta New Testament. For over 50 years, she has taught in Bible fellowships and churches in the United States and other countries, using insight from her understanding of the Biblical languages. Many articles and teachings of interest are available at www.lightofword.org, the Light of the Word Ministry website.

In 1990, Jan began compiling a database of the Aramaic Peshitta New Testament. As computer technology increased over the years, she expanded and developed the database to generate a series of research tools to study the New Testament. The searchable database is available online at www.aramaicdb.org. The *Aramaic Peshitta New Testament Translation* was the first book published in 2006 of a complete *Aramaic Peshitta New Testament Library*. The library includes an interlinear, lexicon, concordance and parallel translations. There is an app of the Aramaic translation on both Apple and Google Play, as well as various electronic versions of her books and the translation.

Jan has also authored several topical books on Biblical subjects: *Enriched in Everything* about giving, *Members in Particular* about the body of Christ, *The Armor of Victory* about the armor of God, *The Coming of the Son of Man* about the sequence of events of the end times, *Ephesians Our Spiritual Treasure*, a workbook on Ephesians and *Our Walk in Christ*.

She lives in Colorado Springs, Colorado.

www.ingramcontent.com/pod-product-compliance
Lightning Source LLC
Chambersburg PA
CBHW071816090426
42737CB00012B/2107